BIBLICA ET ORIENTALIA

(SACRA SCRIPTURA ANTIQUITATIBUS ORIENTALIBUS ILLUSTRATA)

45

biblica et orientalia - 45

ROBERT ALTHANN

STUDIES IN NORTHWEST SEMITIC

EDITRICE PONTIFICIO ISTITUTO BIBLICO — ROMA 1997

ISBN 88-7653-348-6

Editrice Pontificio Istituto Biblico
Piazza della Pilotta 35 – Roma, Italia

Aan die lid van die
Ou-Testamentiese Werkgemeenskap van Suid-Afrika
en die
Suider-Afrikaanse Vereniging vir Semitistiek

Acknowledgements

Earlier versions of some of the chapters of this monograph have been read at a variety of academic meetings and I should like to acknowledge with gratitude the comments of colleagues. That on *Prepositions* was delivered at the 1993 Congress of *The Old Testament Society of Southern Africa*, held at the University of Stellenbosch, 16-17 September. It was subsequently published in the *Journal of Northwest Semitic Languages* 20/2 (1994) 179-191. Versions of the chapter on the *Third Person Suffix in -y* were read at the XV. Congress of *The International Organization for the Study of the Old Testament*, held at St John's College, Cambridge 16-21 July 1995 and at the Congress of *The Old Testament Society of Southern Africa*, held at the University of Stellenbosch 3-5 September 1996. An earlier form of the section on *Particles* was read as a paper at the Congress of *The Old Testament Society of Southern Africa*, held at the University of Port Elizabeth, 19-21 September 1995. I should like here to express my appreciation to this Society as also to *The Southern African Society for Semitics*, both of which extended membership to me. To them this work is dedicated. Constructive criticism and encouragement, a friendly atmosphere and outstanding hospitality have made it a pleasure to attend their meetings. Outside of the formal congresses these same characteristics have made memorable my visits to colleagues in the different South African universities. A special word of thanks is due to the members and staff of the Department of Ancient Near Eastern Studies at the University of Stellenbosch, who always made me welcome in the Department and generously made available their electronic and library facilities. I should also like to thank the staff of the following libraries for their helpfulness which enabled me to profit from their fine facilities over the years: the J.S. Gericke-biblioteek and the library of the Kweekskool in Stellenbosch, and the library of the Pontifical Biblical Institute in Rome.

I further express appreciation to my colleague, Fr A. Gianto S.J., Professor of Semitic Languages and Linguistics in the Faculty of Ancient Near Eastern Studies at this Institute and editor of *Biblica et Orientalia*. It was he who suggested the topic as one appropriate to the series. His careful reading of earlier drafts and penetrating comments greatly improved the work. At the same time I take full responsibility for the opinions expressed. Lastly I thank superiors and confreres in the Society of Jesus for their steady support.

Contents

Abbreviations

The abbreviations employed in this work are basically those found in *Biblica*'s 'Instructions for Contributors'. An asterisk indicates a reconstructed form. In addition, the following abbreviations are used:

BL	*Historische Grammatik der hebräischen Sprache des Alten Testamentes*, H. Bauer and P. Leander
*CML*²	*Canaanite Myths and Legends*, ed. J.C.L. Gibson
DCH	*The Dictionary of Classical Hebrew*, ed. D.J.A. Clines
DISI	*Dictionary of the North-West Semitic Inscriptions*, eds. J. Hoftijzer and K. Jongeling
f.	feminine
GesB	*Hebräisches und aramäisches Handwörterbuch über das Alte Testament*, ed. W. Gesenius and F. Buhl
JB	*Jerusalem Bible*
KTU	*The Cuneiform Alphabetic Texts from Ugarit, Ras Ibn Hani and Other Places*, eds. M. Dietrich, O. Loretz and J. Sanmartín
m.	masculine
Martinez, *Index*	*Hebrew-Ugaritic Index to the Writings of Mitchell J. Dahood*, I and II, E.R. Martinez
MLC	*Mitos y leyendas de Canaan según la tradición de Ugarit*, G. del Olmo Lete
NIV	*New International Version*
NJB	*New Jerusalem Bible*
NRSV	*New Revised Standard Version*

pl.	plate
REB	*Revised English Bible*
RSP	*Ras Shamra Parallels* I-II, ed. L.R. Fisher, III, ed. S. Rummel
RV	*Revised Version*
s.	singular
SEL	*Studi Epigrafici e Linguistici*
TOML	*Textes ougaritiques: Mythes et légendes*, tr. A. Caquot, M. Sznycer and A. Herdner
TOTRR	*Textes ougaritiques: Textes religieux et rituels*, tr. A. Caquot and J.-M. de Tarragon
WBC	Word Biblical Commentary
WOC	*An Introduction to Biblical Hebrew Syntax*, B.K. Waltke and M. O'Connor
ZAH	*Zeitschrift für Althebraistik*
ZLH	*Lexicon Hebraicum et Aramaicum Veteris Testamenti*, ed. F. Zorell

1
Introduction

1. The Premises

The given Biblical Hebrew texts are restricted in volume. They were written in a consonantal script which slowly developed a limited system of *matres lectionis* for indicating vowels. The full vocalisation of the received text goes back only to the Middle Ages and is the work of the Massoretes. These scholars were following a tradition when they introduced their system of vocalisation into the biblical text. Nevertheless, this tradition had not remained unchanged.

At the same time the biblical books were written over a considerable span of time during which grammatical forms underwent changes. The final editing of the received text took place long after the earlier texts were composed, and the final work as reflected in the received text betrays evidence of this. The Massoretic recension sometimes implies an inferior understanding of the text or even occasionally one that is deemed unacceptable by the consensus of modern scholarly opinion. To construct a grammar of the Hebrew bible is therefore a formidable task. As grammarians have seen, it is clearly impossible to write one without reference to cognate Semitic languages that can provide a wider context within which to view the grammatical and lexical phenomena of the biblical text.

2. The Ancient Versions and Qumran

The oldest witness to the sacred text up to the present time is the translation into Greek, the Septuagint, carried out over a period of time in the third to second centuries B.C. Nevertheless, the relationship of this version to the received Hebrew text is not always clear. In some books it follows the Hebrew closely, in others there are striking differences. The scrolls found at Qumran show that even after the translation of the Septuagint, different Hebrew texts of the biblical books existed side by side, some like *1QIsa*[a] in a proto-Massoretic form, others like *1QIsa*[b] closer to the LXX. Proposals for changes in the MT on the basis of the ancient versions or of the Qumran scrolls are unlikely to carry conviction until the nature of the relationship between the different text forms is established.

3. The Problem of Method

To overcome the limitations posed by the comparatively small corpus of biblical texts, Mitchell Dahood situated them in a wider context. The discovery of literary texts at Ras Shamra-Ugarit had disclosed the existence of a language closely related to Biblical Hebrew. Dahood's own studies in Ugaritic and Hebrew convinced him that both languages were in fact merely dialects of Northwest Semitic in which he also included Phoenician-Punic. As a result he felt free to move between these different tongues and explain phenomena in one in the light of another. Not that he was insensitive to the nuances peculiar to Biblical Hebrew, Ugaritic and Phoenician. He took account of them, but it must be admitted more when they furthered his interpretation of a passage than when the opposite was the case.

With regard to the text, Dahood insisted especially on two points. First, he maintained the sanctity of the consonantal text and very rarely resorted to its emendation.[1] Secondly, he argued that the Massoretes failed to appreciate the characteristics of older Hebrew poetry:

> The reverence of the Masoretes for the consonantal text outstripped their knowledge of archaic Hebrew poetry: the result is that their vocalization, and even their word division, must sometimes be disregarded if one is to find the way back to the original sense.[2]

Dahood did not deny the existence of 'a strong tradition of prayer and singing which secured the pronunciation of the psalms even when the grammatical parsing of forms was not immediately evident'.[3] None the less, he never accorded the Massoretic vowels the respect he granted the consonants.

The view that Biblical Hebrew, Ugaritic and Phoenician were only dialectally distinct is generally rejected. This of course does not mean that difficulties in Biblical Hebrew cannot be illuminated by reference to Ugaritic, but more caution needs to be exercised and the context with its literary form considered. A criticism made of Dahood's work in general is precisely that he paid too little attention to the wider context of a passage.[4] As a result, while individual suggestions might prove acceptable, the method as a whole did not find widespread approval. It is therefore necessary to consider each proposal for a new reading of the MT on its own merits.

The aim of the present study is to investigate a number of grammatical phenomena observed by Dahood with a view to establishing how far his answers fit the context of the passages in question and to what extent his solutions improve on those proposed by other scholars.

---

[1] Cf. M. Dahood, *Psalms* I 1-50. Introduction, Translation, and Notes (AB 16; Doubleday: Garden City 1966) xx-xxii.

[2] Dahood, *Psalms* I, xxii.

[3] Dahood, *Psalms* I, xxiii.

[4] Barr, 'Philology and exegesis: some general remarks, with illustrations from Job 3,' BETL 33 (1974) 39-61, esp. 44, 58-59.

2
Approaches to Prepositions in Northwest Semitic Studies

1. Meaning and Translation

Mitchell Dahood was fond of quoting the opening lines of the chapter on prepositions in C.H. Gordon's *Ugaritic Textbook*, "The most interesting feature of Ugar. prepositions is the meaning 'from' for both *b* and *l*. The ambiguity of *b* and *l* is troublesome in reading Ugar.: *b* is either 'in(to), by, with' or 'from', while *l* is either 'to, for' or 'from'. However, even in the O.T., Heb. *la-* and *ba-* sometimes mean 'from'."[1] There is today widespread agreement among Old Testament scholars that these two prepositions are sometimes to be rendered 'from',[2] but the fact that a Hebrew preposition may require different translations does not necessarily

[1] Gordon, *UT* 92 (#10.1); M. Dahood, 'Can One Plow without Oxen? (Amos 6:12): A Study of *ba-* and *'al*,' in *The Bible World: Essays in Honor of Cyrus H. Gordon* (ed. G. Rendsburg et al.) (Ktav: New York 1980) 13. In place of 'ambiguity' which implies that both meanings appear simultaneously it might be better to employ 'ambivalence'. See R. Meyer, 'Gegensinn und Mehrdeutigkeit in der althebräischen Wort- und Begriffsbildung,' *UF* 11 (1979) 606-610.

[2] M.D. Futato, 'The Preposition "Beth" in the Hebrew Psalter,' *WTJ* 41 (1978-1979) 68-83.

imply that it has different *meanings*.[3] It may simply be the idiomatic way of saying something in the language. A classical example occurs in Gen 44,5, הֲלוֹא זֶה אֲשֶׁר יִשְׁתֶּה אֲדֹנִי בּוֹ, rendered by the RSV, 'Is it not *from* this that my lord drinks'? The RV offered, '*in* which,' but few would find this acceptable today. Another instance occurs in Amos 6,6, הַשֹּׁתִים בְּמִזְרְקֵי יַיִן, translated by the RSV, 'who drink wine in bowls', but by the NRSV, 'who drink wine from bowls', which is surely what the Hebrew intended.[4] The usual idiom in Hebrew employs the preposition מן. On the other hand, it is not necessary to conclude that ב here necessarily *means* 'from', that is designates the direction from the point of origin. In Judg 7,6 וַיְהִי מִסְפַּר הַמְלַקְקִים בְּיָדָם אֶל־פִּיהֶם שְׁלֹשׁ מֵאוֹת, 'And the number of those that lapped, putting their hands to their mouths, was three hundred men' (RSV), the ב in the syntagm לקק ב is more plausibly explained as instrumental rather than as indicating the direction. The ב in Gen 44,5 and Amos 6,6 may then also be classified as instrumental.[5] The Italian idiom employed in Gen 44,5 is 'la coppa in cui beve'. The perspective of Italian here is to consider the location whereas English views the action. In other cases it may be the perspective of author rather than language that needs to be divined. In Psalm 46,2, for instance, whether עֶזְרָה בְצָרוֹת is to be understood as, 'liberator from

[3] E.F. Sutcliffe, 'A Note on *ʿal*, *le*, and *from*,' *VT* 5 (1955) 436-439; W.L. Moran, 'The Hebrew Language in Its Northwest Semitic Background,' *The Bible and the Ancient Near East*. Essays in honor of William Foxwell Albright (ed. G.E. Wright) (Doubleday: Garden City 1961) 69 n.70; J. Barr, *Comparative Philology and the Text of the Old Testament* (Clarendon: Oxford 1968) 177; D.G. Pardee, 'The Preposition in Ugaritic (Part I),' *UF* 7 (1975) 329-378, esp. 335; J.H. Hospers, 'Das Problem der sogenannten semantischen Polarität im Althebräischen,' *ZAH* 1 (1988) 32-39, esp. 34; E. Jenni, *Die hebräischen Präpositionen*, Band 1: *Die Präposition Beth* (Kohlhammer: Stuttgart 1992) 16.

[4] Cf. W.R. Harper, *A Critical and Exegetical Commentary on Amos and Hosea* (ICC; T. & T. Clark: Edinburgh 1904) 150.

[5] Cf. Jenni, *Präposition Beth*, 127 n.190.

sieges'[6] or as 'help in (time of) trouble'[7] would seem to depend on the perspective of the author. This would be an example of ambiguity which, however, may derive from the lexical meaning of the two nouns rather than from ב. The cognate verb in Ugaritic, *ʿḏr* followed by *b* clearly has the translation value of 'save from' in KTU 1.18(3 Aqht).I:14 *wyʿḏrk.b yd.btlt.[ʿnt]*, 'He will save you from the hand of maiden Anat'. A factor in deciding on the translation would therefore also be one's view of the relationship between Ugaritic and Hebrew.

An analogous situation obtains in Akkadian where *ina*, normally to be rendered 'in, on, through,' can require the translation, 'from'.[8] In some El Amarna letters from Canaanite regions the Akkadian preposition *ištu* which carries the sense of 'from, out of, since, after, by'[9] may demand different renderings. Thus EA 136:26 *imluk ištu libbīja alikmi*, 'I thought to myself, "Come!"' EA 147:15 *t[a]r-gu₅-ub gabbi māti ištu rigmīšu*, 'and all the land is frightened at his cry'.[10]

2. The Prepositions ב, מן, ל, על

G. Schmuttermayr points out that there are passages where the 'unusual' use of Hebrew prepositions is found in archaic material.[11] This seems to be the case in Psalm 18 - 2 Samuel 22 whose text has come down in two versions. In v. 14 we read: וַיַּרְעֵם בַּשָּׁמַיִם יְהוָה (Ps

[6] M. Dahood, *Psalms* III 101-150. Introduction, Translation, and Notes (AB 17A; Doubleday: Garden City 1970) XXVI.

[7] D. Pardee, 'Attestations of Ugaritic Verb/Preposition Combinations in Later Dialects,' *UF* 9 (1977) 223.

[8] *CAD* 7, 142; *AHw* 1, 380.

[9] Cf. *CAD* 7, 286; *AHw* 1, 401.

[10] Cf. W.L. Moran, *The Amarna Letters* (Johns Hopkins University Press: Baltimore - London 1992) 217, 233.

[11] G. Schmuttermayr, 'Ambivalenz und Aspektdifferenz. Bemerkungen zu den hebräischen Präpositionen ב, ל und מן,' *BZ* N.F. 15 (1971) 29-51, esp. 46.

18) 'And YHWH thundered from[12] (or: in[13]) heaven'; יַרְעֵם מִן־שָׁמַיִם יְהוָה (2 Sam 22) 'And YHWH thundered from heaven'. Parallel expressions are found in Ugaritic literature, thus KTU 1.4(51).V:8(70), *w tn.qlh.b ʿrpt*, 'And he gives forth his voice in[14] [or: from[15]] the clouds'. Some scholars believe that the use of two different prepositions in the parallel biblical passages reflects a difference in perspective, so that Ps 18,14 should be rendered, 'And YHWH thundered in heaven'.[16] On the other hand the fact that there is evidence for a number of grammatical revisions in 2 Samuel 22 suggests that the difference may be merely grammatical and not semantic. The 'old' preposition ב has been 'modernized' to מן.[17] In v. 16c-d the same phenomenon appears, albeit semantically different, and now it is 2 Samuel 22 that employs ב:

בְּגַעֲרַת יְהוָה מִנִּשְׁמַת רוּחַ אַפּוֹ
at the rebuke of YHWH,
at the blast of the breath of his nostrils. (2 Sam 22,16)

מִגַּעֲרָתְךָ יְהוָה מִנִּשְׁמַת רוּחַ אַפֶּךָ

[12] Cf. NAB, NIV, NJB (as JB), REB (as NEB).

[13] Cf. NRSV (as RSV).

[14] A. Schoors, 'Literary Phrases,' *RSP* I, 1-70, see 23-24 [but Dahood's explanation of *wtn* as a possible syncope of *wytn* may still be preferable, cf. S.E. Loewenstamm, 'Ugarit and the Bible. I,' *Bib* 76 (1975) 103-119, on 107]; *TOML*, 208; D.G. Pardee, 'The Preposition in Ugaritic (Part II),' *UF* 8 (1976) 215-322, see 241-242; *CML*², 60.

[15] Cf. *MLC*, 202.

[16] C. Brekelmans, 'Some Considerations on the Translation of the Psalms by M. Dahood. I The Preposition *b=from* in the Psalms According to M. Dahood,' *UF* 1 (1969) 5-14, esp. 8-9; Schoors, 'Literary Phrases,' 23-24; Pardee, 'The Preposition in Ugaritic', *UF* 8 (1976) 241-242. See too NRSV.

[17] G. Schmuttermayr, *Psalm 18 und 2 Samuel 22*. Studien zu einem Doppeltext. Probleme der Textkritik und Übersetzung und das Psalterium Pianum (StANT 25; Kösel: München 1971) 76.

at your rebuke, O YHWH,
at the blast of the breath of your nostrils. (Ps 18,16)

In v. 16c there is variation between ב and מן, but in v. 16d both traditions employ מן. There is here no palpable difference of meaning between ב and מן.[18] At the same time there are a number of cases where the ketib offers ב but the qere מן:[19]

K הַרְחֵק מְאֹד בָאָדָם; Q הַרְחֵק מְאֹד מֵאָדָם
very far from Adam. (Josh 3,16)

The Vulgate reads *procul ab urbe quae vocatur Adom*, supporting the understanding of the qere. The LXX has a different text.

K בְּעֵבֶר הַנָּהָר
in the land beyond the River.
Q מֵעֵבֶר הַנָּהָר
from the land beyond the River. (Josh 24,15)

There may be a difference of perspective:

Q: either the gods whom your ancestors worshipped, who were *from* the land beyond (מֵעֵבֶר) the River.
K: either the gods whom your ancestors worshipped, who were *in* the land beyond (בְּעֵבֶר) the River.

The LXX renders ἐν τῷ πέραν τοῦ ποταμοῦ, the Vulgate *in Mesopotamia*, both this time supporting the ketib.

---

[18] Cf. Schmuttermayr, *Psalm 18*, 76, 84.
[19] Schmuttermayr, 'Ambivalenz', *BZ* N.F. 15 (1971) 43-44.

The opposite phenomenon where the ketib offers מן but the qere ב is also observable:

K מֵעֵבֶר הַיַּרְדֵּן, Q בְּעֵבֶר הַיַּרְדֵּן
in the land beyond the Jordan. (Josh 22,7)

Here מן requires to be translated, 'in'. This too is the understanding of the LXX ἐν τῷ πέραν τοῦ Ιορδάνου, and of the Vulgate *(inter ceteros fratres suos) trans Jordanem.* A similar rendering is desirable in some other passages:

עַם־רַב הֹלְכִים מִדֶּרֶךְ
(and he saw) a lot of people walking on the road.
LXX λαὸς πολὺς πορευόμενος ἐν τῇ ὁδῷ.
Vulgate *populus multus veniebat per iter.* (2 Sam 13,34)

וַיִּקַּח דָּוִד עוֹד פִּלַגְשִׁים וְנָשִׁים מִירוּשָׁלַםִ
And David again took concubines and wives in Jerusalem.
LXX ἐξ Ιερουσαλημ.
Vulgate *de Hierusalem.* (2 Sam 5,13a)[20]

This apparent alternation of ב and מן raises the question of the relationship between the two prepositions. A number of verbs are followed by either ב or מן without apparent difference in meaning. A similar variation may be found between ל and מן:[21]

לֹא יִמְנַע־טוֹב לַהֹלְכִים בְּתָמִים

[20] The parallel in 1 Chr 14,3 reads בירושלם. Cf. Schmuttermayr, 'Ambivalenz', *BZ* 15 (1971) 45 and n. 93.

[21] Schmuttermayr, 'Ambivalenz', *BZ* 15 (1971) 43.

He does not withhold the good thing[22] from those
who walk with integrity.[23] (Ps 84,12)

אַל־תִּמְנַע־טוֹב מִבְּעָלָיו
Withhold not pay from those working for it.[24] (Prov 3,27)

עֲצָרַנִי יְהוָה מִלֶּדֶת
YHWH prevented me from bearing. (Gen 16,2)

אַל־תַּעֲצָר־לִי לִרְכֹּב
Do not prevent me from riding.[25] (2 Kgs 4,24)

In Ugaritic *l* performs a variety of functions.[26] It requires the translation 'from' in KTU 1.6.I:64(49.I:36):

(63) *yrd* (64) *l kḥṯ.aliyn.bʿl*,
He descends from the throne of Aliyan Baal.[27]

---

22 טוֹב may here carry the connotation, 'rain'. Cf. M. Dahood, *Psalms* II 51-100. Introduction, Translation, and Notes (AB 17; Doubleday: Garden City ²1973) 283. Consult also, though without mention of this verse, O. Loretz, 'Ugaritisch *ṭbn* und hebräisch *ṭwb* "Regen". Regenrituale beim Neujahrfest in Kanaan und Israel (Ps 85; 126),' *UF* 21 (1989) 247-258.

23 Cf. *UT* 92 (#10.1).

24 M. Dahood, *Proverbs and Northwest Semitic Philology* (Scripta Pontificii Instituti Biblici 113; Pontificium Institutum Biblicum: Roma 1963) 10-11; C.F. Whitley, 'Some Functions of the Hebrew Particles *beth* and *lamedh*,' *JQR* 62 (1971-1972) 206 and n.29.

25 Cf. Gordon, *UT*, 92 (#10.1) with further examples; G.A. Rendsburg, 'Morphological Evidence for Regional Dialects in Ancient Hebrew,' *Linguistics and Biblical Hebrew* (ed. W. Bodine) (Eisenbrauns: Winona Lake 1992) 65-88, esp. 81. Dahood has proposed numerous biblical examples of ל, 'from,' cf. Martinez, *Index* I, 117, II, 128.

26 Gordon, *UT*, 97-99 (#10.10-11).

27 For other examples of *yrd l*, 'descend from,' cf. Pardee, 'The Preposition in Ugaritic', *UF* 7 (1975) 350.

On the other hand, 'to' is the rendering in KTU 1.15(128).III:18-19:

> *tity.ilm.l ahlhm* (19) *dr il. l mšknthm,*
> the gods go to their tents,
> the assembly of El to their dwellings.

In Phoenician too the prepositions *b* and *l* can indicate, 'from':

> KAI 14.5-6 *w'l y'm*(6)*sn bmškb z 'lt mškb šny,*
> And he may not carry me from this resting place
> of mine to another resting place.[28]

Another preposition which sometimes requires the translation 'from' is עַל, for instance Ps 81,6:

> בְּצֵאתוֹ עַל־אֶרֶץ מִצְרָיִם
> when he went from the land of Egypt.[29]

For Ugaritic the situation is less clear, as the following text shows:

> *isp špš l hrm ǵrpl*
> *'l arṣ lan isp ḥmt* (KTU 1.107:32-33.34-35.37-38)

---

[28] Cf. S. Segert, *A Grammar of Phoenician and Punic* (Beck: München 1976) 206 (#66.221); María-José Fuentes Estañol, *Vocabulario Fenicio* (Biblioteca Fenicia 1; Consejo Superior de Investigaciones Científicas: Barcelona 1980) 79; *DISI* I, 138 d). See too *KAI* 5:2 *bmṣrm*, 'from Egypt' (*KAI* II, 7); *DISI* I, 139 line 2).

[29] Cf. *HALAT*, 782a 7; Sutcliffe, 'A Note', *VT* 5 (1955) 437; M. Dietrich - O. Loretz, 'Die bipolare Position von *'l* im Ugaritischen und Hebräischen,' *UF* 18 (1986) 449-450.

Enlève, Sha]pash, *sans relâche*, l'obscurité au-dessus de la terre, la force du venin (enlève-la)... (Caquot)[30]

Tu recueilles, *Ša]pšu*, sur les montagnes la nuée,
Sur la terre du Fort recueille le venin. (Pardee)[31]

Nimm, Sonne, von den Bergen das Wolkendunkel,
von der Erde, o Starker, nimm das Gift! (Dietrich - Loretz)[32]

Caquot and Pardee understand *ʿl* in the sense of 'above' but take different views of the stichometry. Pardee sees the text as a bicolon, Caquot does not. Dietrich and Loretz also see a bicolon here and argue that in view of the parallel between *l hrm ǵrpl* and *ʿl arṣ...ḥmt*, 'von den Bergen das Wolkendunkel' / 'von der Erde...das Gift', *ʿl* carries a separative connotation. The context is unfortunately damaged and how the passage is to be understood and its precise translation remain a matter of judgment.

An example of *ʿl* requiring the translation 'from' can be found in the Phoenician Aḥiram inscription, KAI 1.2:

wnḥt tbrḥ ʿl gbl,
May calm flee from Byblos.[33]

It is probably also present in the Mesha inscription from Moab, KAI 181.14:

---

30 *TOTRR*, 99.

31 D. Pardee, *Les textes para-mythologiques: de la 24ᵉ campagne (1961)* (Mémoire 77; Recherche sur les Civilisations: Paris 1988) 241.

32 See Dietrich - Loretz, 'Die bipolare Position', *UF* 18 (1986) 449-450.

33 KAI 1.2, see *KAI* II, 2; Segert, *A Grammar of Phoenician*, 207 (#66.223); R.S. Tomback, *A Comparative Semitic Lexicon of the Phoenician and Punic Languages* (SBLDS 32; Missoula: Scholars 1978) 244; *DISI* II, 847ε).

lk ʾḥz ʾt nbh ʿl yśrʾl,

KAI II, 169 renders, 'Geh, nimm Nebo (im Kampf) gegen Israel!', but this seems forced. *DISI* I, 36 remarks that עַל carries a negative implication, against, but translates 'from Israel'. This rendering is required by the context, 'Go, take Nebo from Israel'.[34]

Some scholars have explained this ambivalence in the use of some prepositions as due to 'interchangeability': one preposition may be employed in place of another.[35] Complete interchangeability is hardly possible since the function of prepositions is to indicate the nature of a relationship.[36] An overlap in the semantic fields is another matter. In the case of Hebrew ב and מן there is, however, a special factor involved. The study of texts in Ugaritic has up to now failed to elicit any examples of *m(n)*, 'from,' in the poetic texts and

---

[34] Cf. S. Segert, 'Die Sprache der moabitischen Königsinschrift,' *ArOr* 29 (1961) 197-267, on 228 #4:742; F.I. Andersen, 'Moabite Syntax,' *Or* n.s. 35 (1966) 81-120; J.C.L. Gibson, *Textbook of Syrian Semitic Inscriptions* Volume I *Hebrew and Moabite Inscriptions* (Clarendon: Oxford 1971, 1973) 76; Schmuttermayr, *BZ* N.F. 15 (1971) 37; M. Dahood, 'The Moabite Stone and Northwest Semitic Philology,' *The Archaeology of Jordan and Other Studies.* Presented to Siegfried H. Horn (ed. L.T. Geraty - L.G. Herr) (Andrews University Press: Berrien Springs 1986) 429-441, on 433-434; Kent P. Jackson, 'The Language of the Meshaʿ Inscription', *Studies in the Mesha Inscription and Moab* (ed. A. Dearman) (Archaeology and Biblical Studies 2; Scholars: Atlanta 1989) 96-130, esp. 114.

[35] N. Sarna, 'The Interchange of the prepositions *Beth* and *Min* in Biblical Hebrew,' *JBL* 78 (1959) 310-316; M. Dahood, *Ugaritic-Hebrew Philology.* Marginal Notes on Recent Publications (BibOr 17; Pontifical Biblical Institute: Rome 1965) 26-27; W. Chomsky, 'The Ambiguity of the Prefixed Prepositions מ, ל, ב in the Bible', *JQR* 61 (1970-1971) 87-89; Whitley, *JQR* (1971-1972) 199-206.

[36] *WOC*, 187 (#11.1); Jenni, *Präposition Beth,* 12.

only one highly disputed example in the prose.[37] It is not unlikely that the earliest Hebrew showed a similar lack[38] and that מן was only gradually introduced into the language. If this is so then ב would have had at least some of the functions later exercised by מן. G.A. Rendsburg has suggested that מן may in fact be a late development in the language.[39] He notes that Z. Zevit has argued that Phoenician did not have *m(n)* until the fourth century B.C.[40] and tentatively suggests that the same may have been true for Israelian (Northern) Hebrew.[41] It is in any case possible, especially with parallel traditions and duplicate texts, that the differences are sometimes dialectal or regional. Yet there may be instances of a genuinely old text whose second version shows signs of being a revision. The more 'usual' preposition replaced the 'unusual,' but there may have been a sufficient overlapping in the semantic fields of the prepositions to allow their use in parallel for the sake of variety in style or for some other reason.[42]

---

[37] KTU 2.16(1015):11 has been suggested, see conveniently Schmuttermayr, 'Ambivalenz', *BZ* 15 (1971) 32 and n.18, but another interpretation is possible, cf. M. Dietrich - O. Loretz, 'Zweifelhafte Belege für *m(n)* "von". Zur ugaritischen Lexikographie (XVI),' *UF* 12 (1980) 183-187, esp. 185-186; E. Lipiński, 'Aḫat-Milki, reine d'Ugarit, et la guerre de Mukiš,' *OLP* 12 (1981) 97-99; D.G. Pardee, 'The Preposition in Ugaritic (Part II), *UF* 8 (1976) 270; id., 'Ugaritic: Further Studies in Ugaritic Epistolography', *AfO* 31 (1984) 213-230, on 221.

[38] Cf. Pardee, 'The Preposition in Ugaritic', *UF* 8 (1976) 312.

[39] 'Morphological Evidence', 80.

[40] Z. Zevit, 'The So-Called Interchangeability of the Prepositions *b, l, and m(n)* in Northwest Semitic,' *JANES* 7 (1975) 103-112, esp. 107-109.

[41] On 'northern' Hebrew, see also Françoise Briguel-Chatonnet, 'Hébreu du Nord et Phénicien: Étude comparée de deux dialectes cananéens,' *OLP* 23 (1992) 89-126; I. Young, 'The "Northernisms" of the Israelite Narratives in Kings,' *ZAH* 8/1 (1995) 63-70; D.C. Fredericks, 'A North Israelite Dialect in the Hebrew Bible? Questions of Methodology', *Hebrew Studies* 37 (1996) 7-20: the 'northernisms' may in fact be merely colloquialisms.

[42] See Schmuttermayr, 'Ambivalenz', *BZ* 15 (1971) 46.

The fact that ב or ל and מן can be employed apparently interchangeably would seem to imply a *certain fluctuation* in the meaning of these prepositions. This is the position of Gordon, Sarna, Whitley, Dahood, Schmuttermayr, Rendsburg. On the other hand D. Pardee in his study of the semantic fields of Ugaritic prepositions concludes that prepositions have 'one basic meaning'.[43] Variations are 'due to the nature of the verb used with the preposition, to the perspective of the author, and to idiomatic development of expressions'. By perspective Pardee means 'the author's point of view on the action depicted by a verb/preposition combination' and 'the point in the continuum of action to which the preposition refers in a given language's description of an action, and to the specificity of direction supplied by a language's prepositional system'.[44] Pardee also speaks of *b* in the sense of 'position before movement' or 'from'.[45] He argues that for *b* 'a translation "from" is only possible where the perspective allows for the item in question being, at some time during the time span of the action, in the position indicated by *b*'.[46] After a similar fashion, Pardee describes *l* in terms of position rather than direction: *l* means 'position at,' 'pertaining to,' or 'belonging to'.[47] In other words it is not the preposition by itself that has different meanings. It is rather the circumstances that dictate a particular understanding not just of the preposition but of the whole

---

43 Pardee, 'The Preposition in Ugaritic', *UF* 8 (1976) 286. Consult the authors and references in n.3 above.

44 Pardee, 'The preposition in Ugaritic', *UF* 7 (1975) 335 and *UF* 8 (1976) 282.

45 Pardee, 'The Preposition in Ugaritic', *UF* 8 (1976) 304. See too K. Aartun, *Die Partikeln des Ugaritischen 2. Teil: Präpositionen, Konjunktionen* (AOAT 21/2; Butzon & Bercker: Kevelaer 1978) 1: *b* is employed 'zur Angabe *des räumlichen Verweilens in der unmittelbaren Nähe*'.

46 Pardee, 'The Preposition in Ugaritic', *UF* 8 (1976) 290.

47 Pardee, *UF* 8 (1976) 289. Cf. Aartun, *Partikeln*, 32: *l* is employed to indicate spatial, conceptual or temporal relationships.

expression. This is in fact not so far from the views of Dahood who writes, 'Ugaritic and Hebrew prepositions are semantically very flexible and fluid, *acquiring their specific nuance from the verb with which they are used or from the context*, because not infrequently there is no verb'.[48] It is more in the application of the theory that differences arise. Since it is from Ugaritic that the current debate on prepositions arose,[49] it will be appropriate to consider some examples of apparent ambiguity in Ugaritic prepositions.

Ugaritic *rḥṣ b* may be understood to mean 'wash in' or 'wash from' in KTU 1.3(ʿnt).II:34-35:

> *[t]rḥṣ.ydh.b dm.ḏmr*
> *[u]ṣbʿth.b mmʿ.mhrm*
> She bathes her hands in[50] [or: of[51]] the soldiers' blood
> Her fingers in [or: of] the warriors' gore.

Some light may be thrown on the meaning of this passage by KTU 1.16.VI(127):10:

> *wtṯb.trḥṣ.nn.b dʿt*:
> She returns and washes him when he sweats (or: of sweat).

---

[48] M. Dahood, Review of Aartun, *Partikeln*, in *Or* n.s. 51 (1982) 281 [emphasis added].

[49] Cf. Jenni, *Präposition Beth*, 11.

[50] Cf. Pardee, *UF* 8 (1976) 266-267 (with bibliography).

[51] Cf. M. Dahood, 'Hebrew-Ugaritic Lexicography IX,' *Bib* 52 (1971) 337-356, see 355; *TOML*, 161; *CML*², 48; *MLC*, 182.

The separative nuance of *b* is appropriate here,[52] although a temporal understanding of the line is also possible.[53] Dahood has proposed the same separative translation of the preposition in Ps 58,11, where the usual rendering is 'in':

> יִשְׂמַח צַדִּיק כִּי־חָזָה נָקָם פְּעָמָיו יִרְחַץ בְּדַם הָרָשָׁע
> The just man will rejoice when he beholds his victory,
> He will wash his feet of the blood of the wicked.[54]
> (RSV: He will bathe his feet in the blood of the wicked.)[55]

Either translation is possible and the choice may well be influenced by cultural considerations. Relevant too would be one's view of the relationship between Ugaritic and Hebrew. Another difficult case is KTU 1.2.IV(68):13-14:

> (13) *trtqṣ.bd bʿl.km nš*(14)*r.b uṣbʿth*
> Swoop in the hand of Baal,
> Like an eagle in his fingers. (Pardee)[56]

---

[52] Cf. *TOML*, 570; *CML*², 101; *MLC*, 320.

[53] Pardee, *UF* 7 (1975) 369.

[54] Dahood, *Psalms II*, 56, 63. Gibson refers to this verse at KTU 1.3(ʿnt).II:35, cf. *CML*², 48 n.3.

[55] Brian Doyle justly observes parallelism in the verse: חָזָה//יִרְחַץ and נָקָם//הָרָשָׁע, but this does not settle the question of the nuance of the preposition which he renders 'in'. Cf. B. Doyle, 'Psalm 58: Curse as Voiced Disorientation', *Bijdragen* 57 (1996) 122-148, esp. 127, 133-134.

[56] Pardee, *UF* 7 (1975) 370 and *UF* 8 (1976) 267-268.

It is more usual to take the preposition *b* as separative, 'Do you swoop from Baal's hand, like an eagle from his fingers'.[57] Here again, either translation is possible, but in view of the fact that the weapons seem to be thrown, the second rendering may be preferable.[58]

The choice will probably be influenced by one's idea of the basic meaning of the preposition. If this is considered to be 'position within the confines of',[59] then there will probably be more reluctance to accept a separative nuance than if one accepts the view of Dahood that 'Ugaritic and Hebrew prepositions are semantically very flexible and fluid'. In other words there is the difficulty that if a basic meaning is assumed, then there will be a tendency to force the meaning into contexts which may not be appropriate. On the other hand if several original meanings are assumed, then the peculiar function of a particular preposition will tend to disappear. Barr has pointed out the danger to 'communicative efficiency' in the postulation of quite different original meanings.[60]

There is here, apparently, something of an impasse. Segert avoids the term 'meaning' in relation to prepositions, preferring to speak of their 'function' and of what they 'indicate.' He observes that 'The function of prepositions depends on the other elements of the clause, especially the governing verb, and on the general situation' and that 'The prepositions *b*- and *l*- can indicate direction toward a place, and *b* can also indicate being in a place'. 'Both *b*- and *l*- can also indicate direction from, with respect to place and time'.[61]

---

[57] Cf. *TOML*, 137; *CML*^{2}, 44; *MLC*, 176.

[58] Cf. Karin Reiter, 'Falknerei in Ugarit,' *UF* 22 (1990) 271-278.

[59] Pardee, *UF* 8 (1976) 289.

[60] Barr, *Philology*, 175.

[61] Segert, *Grammar of Ugaritic*, 101-102 (#66.2).

3. Meaning and Perspective: Ernst Jenni

Jenni has, however, made a new proposal with regard to the basic meaning of prepositions. He understands prepositions to be particles which express spatio-temporal and similar relations between two objects.[62] The actual meaning of a preposition is derived from its basic meaning combined with its semantic context.[63] The apparent ambiguity of Hebrew prepositions is due to different perspectives and further, the Hebrew prepositional system is determined by local categories.[64] It can be seen that Jenni here supports the view put forward by Pardee and others that prepositions have a basic meaning and that apparent divergences from it are due to a change of perspective.

Jenni observes that the least determined and so most flexible preposition is ל. Its basic meaning is to indicate a relation in the widest sense and it develops its specific function according to context.[65] The preposition ב is also relational in a wide sense and stands in opposition to ל.[66] ב does not specifically distinguish location and movement which are rather contained in the verb. ב merely expresses the end position of the moved object.[67] The relationship between these two prepositions can be described as opposite or complementary in the sense that ל implies (1) separation where ב connects, and (2) inequality where ב indicates equality.[68]

---

[62] Jenni, *Präposition Beth*, 12. See too F.A. Pennacchietti, 'Appunti per una storia comparata dei sistemi preposizionali semitici', *AION* n.s. 24 (1974) 161-208, esp. 161-182; *WOC*, 187-192 (#11.1-11.2).

[63] Jenni, *Präposition Beth*, 15.

[64] Jenni, *Präposition Beth*, 16, 17.

[65] Jenni, *Präposition Beth*, 20, 24.

[66] Jenni, *Präposition Beth*, 25.

[67] Jenni, *Präposition Beth*, 26.

[68] Jenni, *Präposition Beth*, 31.

Now there are cases where the two prepositions are apparently interchangeable, but Jenni argues that we are dealing here with what are semantically special cases where the two objects are so close in meaning that indication of equality by ב or of inequality by ל can have only minimal consequences.[69] For instance, in Exod 15,10, צָלְלוּ כַּעוֹפֶרֶת בְּמַיִם אַדִּירִים, 'they sank like lead in the mighty waters,' the two quantities 'lead' and 'waters' are very different, but they are both presented as spatial objects and enjoy just sufficient affinity to allow the preposition ב to put them in a local relationship. On the other hand, there are also cases where ב and ל link two objects with different meanings but where the second has the same reference as the first. In Gen 29,28, וַיִּתֶּן־לוֹ אֶת־רָחֵל בִּתּוֹ לְאִשָּׁה, 'and he gave him Rachel his daughter to wife,' both 'Rachel his daughter' and 'wife' refer to the same person but differ in meaning: they are semantically congruent.[70]

Jenni does not discuss the preposition מן which, as has been seen, sometimes exercises functions more usually carried out by ב. He does, however, allude to Ezek 48,29 תַּפִּילוּ מִנַּחֲלָה, 'you shall allot as an inheritance' where he recommends emending מן to ב in line with other occurrences of the idiom.[71] ב is described as *beth essentiae*, expressing the role, status or purpose of a material quantity.[72] Hence if מן were allowed to stand, it too would function in this way. The *beth essentiae* is attested in Ugaritic[73] and Phoenician.[74]

---

69 Jenni, *Präposition Beth*, 33.

70 Jenni, *Präposition Beth*, 34.

71 Jenni, *Präposition Beth*, 36 n.65.

72 Jenni, *Präposition Beth*, 86.

73 Cf. Gordon, *UT*, 94 (#10.4), 370 (#435); id., '"In" of Predication or Equivalence,' *JBL* 100 (1981) 612-613.

74 Cf. S. Segert, *A Grammar of Phoenician and Punic* (Beck: München 1976) 208 (#66.35).

Do Jenni's proposals for the basic meanings of ב and ל help to clarify difficult cases? For ל which is defined as relational in the widest sense, this would seem to be the case.[75] A thorough study is promised for the future.[76] With regard to ב it has been seen that Jenni makes the important point that ב does not specifically distinguish location and movement which are rather contained in the verb. ב merely expresses the end position of the moved object. It does not answer the questions 'whence?', for which מן serves, or 'where to?' for which Hebrew uses אל.[77] When employed in a context of movement it indicates the end position, for example, Gen 37,20, 'Let us throw him into one of (בְּאַחַד) the pits'. It is אֶל which specifies direction and goal, as in v. 22, 'cast him into this pit (אֶל־הַבּוֹר) here in the wilderness'. After a similar fashion, ב can refer to a phase of a movement, as in the phrase עָבַר בְּאֶרֶץ, 'passing through a land'. Jenni, however, doubts that ב can indicate the opening phase of a movement. Thus in the expression שתה ב 'drink out of (a cup)' (see Gen 44,5; Amos 6,6) he considers ב instrumental. It is true that in 2 Sam 12,3 שתה is employed with the preposition מן, but the subject is an animal and the exact location is given. In other cases where a translation with 'from' is required he would see a difference of perspective.

A 'difficult' case of the preposition ב occurs in Amos 6,12, הַיְרֻצוּן בַּסֶּלַע סוּסִים אִם־יַחֲרוֹשׁ בַּבְּקָרִים, rendered by Dahood 'can horses run upon rocks, or can one plow without oxen?' He translates ב, 'without' on the grounds that מן sometimes signifies 'without'[78] and is frequently interchangeable with ב.[79] Jenni on the other hand accepts

[75] For the view that 'The basic senses of *l* are spatial', see *WOC*, 205 (#11.2.10b).

[76] Jenni, *Präposition Beth*, 5.

[77] Jenni, *Präposition Beth*, 26-27.

[78] Cf. *HALAT*, 566a 7b).

[79] Dahood, 'Can One Plow without Oxen?,' 14.

the common emendation of בַּבְּקָרִים to בַּבָּקָר יָם, '(can one plow) the sea with oxen?'[80] because he rejects this view. For Jenni ב basically expresses position, for instance the end position of the moved object[81] but not the opening phase in a continuum of movement, for Hebrew already has מן.[82] As was seen above, a relevant question is that of when מן made its appearance in Hebrew. If this occurred relatively late then one would not necessarily find it in older texts.

The importance of a theory of prepositions for our understanding of the biblical text is evident. At the same time Dahood frequently asserted that we do not yet know what the biblical text contains because so many poetic texts remain untranslated.[83]. There is also the question of the extent to which we have access to ancient Hebrew. Is there a sufficient quantity of text to permit an adequate description of the language? Or should one rely on related dialects, and to what extent? There is obviously plenty of room for different opinions on these matters. Careful theoretical work is indispensable for an ordered approach to the subject of prepositions in the Northwest Semitic dialects. On the other hand, the comparatively limited quantity of available ancient Hebrew text makes difficult any description of the language done without reference to related dialects. There is therefore scope for the pragmatic approach which focuses on

---

[80] Jenni, *Präposition Beth*, 121 n.164. For other emendations, cf. A. Cooper, 'The Absurdity of Amos 6.12a,' *JBL* 107 (1988) 725-727; O. Loretz, 'Amos vi 12,' *VT* 39 (1989) 240-242.

[81] Jenni, *Präposition Beth*, 26.

[82] Jenni, *Präposition Beth*, 27.

[83] Dahood, 'Can One Plow without Oxen?,' 19. Healey remarks that Dahood's reluctance to provide synthesis may have been a positive decision on his part, see J.F. Healey, 'The Immortality of the King: Ugarit and the Psalms,' in *Memorial Mitchell J. Dahood*. *Or* n.s. 53 (1984) 245-254, esp. 245.

individual texts and attempts to illuminate them by reference to the practice of cognate languages.

3
On verbal forms: the case of **taqtul*

1. Deuteronomy and Major Prophets

The grammar of Waltke and O'Connor deems the existence of a third masculine singular imperfect *taqtul* in Hebrew 'problematic'.[1] On the other hand studies by H.J. van Dijk and M. Dahood have claimed that this morpheme does indeed exist.[2] A re-examination of the cases put forward by these scholars may therefore be appropriate.[3]

וְדַם־עֵנָב תִּשְׁתֶּה־חָמֶר (Deut 32,14)
And of the blood of the grape you drank wine. (RSV)

And the blood of the grape he drank by the vat. (Dahood)[4]

The reason why Dahood postulates a third person verb in this verse is that the previous verses employ the third person. V. 14 ends the pericope and might be expected to witness the same person.

---

[1] *WOC*, 497 n.2. See too A. Schoors, 'A Third Masculine Singular *taqtul* in Biblical Hebrew?' *Text and Context*. Old Testament and Semitic Studies for F.C. Fensham (ed. W. Claassen) (JSOTSS 48; JSOT: Sheffield 1988) 193-200.

[2] Cf. H.J. van Dijk, 'Does third masculine singular **taqtul* exist in Hebrew,' *VT* 19 (1969) 440-447; M. Dahood, 'Third Masculine Singular with Preformative *t-* in Northwest Semitic,' *Or* n.s. 48 (1979) 97-106 and Martinez, *Index* II, 133.

[3] In general only those cases will be considered that do not involve changes to the MT.

[4] Dahood, *Or* n.s. 48 (1979) 98.

Nevertheless, a closer look at the whole passage discloses an alternation of person. V. 7 begins the section with an address in the second person. The following verses employ the third person, and then v. 14 which concludes the section ends with the second person, in this way effecting an inclusion. From the literary standpoint, the second person is therefore preferable to the third. The Vulgate renders *biberet* and the LXX ἔπιον, 'he drank', but these are probably facilitating readings and so, despite this support for the third person, the second person may be retained.[5]

> בַּיּוֹם הַהוּא יְגַלַּח אֲדֹנָי בְּתַעַר הַשְּׂכִירָה בְּעֶבְרֵי נָהָר
> בְּמֶלֶךְ אַשּׁוּר אֶת־הָרֹאשׁ וְשַׂעַר הָרַגְלָיִם וְגַם אֶת־הַזָּקָן תִּסְפֶּה (Isa 7,20)
>
> In that day the Lord will shave with a razor which is hired beyond the River—with the king of Assyria—the head and the hair of the feet, and it will sweep away the beard also. (RSV)
>
> The Lord will shave with a hired razor...the head and the hair of the feet and he will sweep away the beard also. (Van Dijk)[6]

The RSV takes the subject of תִּסְפֶּה to be תַעַר, apparently assuming that the noun is feminine in this instance, although masculine in Num 6,5. Van Dijk points out, however, that one would rather expect the subject to be 'the Lord' as it is for יְגַלַּח (see Gen 18,23-24). The Massoretes either understand תַעַר הַשְּׂכִירָה to be a construct phrase which can be followed by a feminine verb, or they take הַשְּׂכִירָה to be

[5] See too S.R. Driver, *A Critical and Exegetical Commentary on Deuteronomy* (ICC; T. & T. Clark: Edinburgh [3]1901) 360; Schoors, '*Taqtul*', 195 and n.23.

[6] Van Dijk, *VT* 19 (1969) 445.

in apposition.[7] The grammatical subject would then be the feminine הַשְּׂכִירָה, understood as an abstract noun with a concrete meaning: 'mercenaries'.[8] One could in other words see here an instance of a word developing a second meaning from the context, the sense of 'hired' from its proximity to 'razor' changing to 'mercenaries' with the verb תִּסְפֶּה.[9] The feminine verb is consequently appropriate to the context and there is no need to assume the existence of **taqtul*.

עַל אַדְמַת עַמִּי קוֹץ שָׁמִיר תַּעֲלֶה
כִּי עַל־כָּל־בָּתֵּי מָשׂוֹשׂ קִרְיָה עַלִּיזָה (Isa 32,13)
(V. 12 Beat upon your breasts...)
for the soil of my people growing up in thorns and briers;
yea, for all the joyous houses in the joyful city. (RSV)

Upon the soil of my people thorns, briers spring up,
yea upon all the houses of mirth, the festive city itself. (Dahood)[10]

The verb תַּעֲלֶה looks like a feminine form and so the subject would appear to be אַדְמַת עַמִּי. Nevertheless, one might expect the thorns

---

[7] Cf. G.B. Gray, *A Critical and Exegetical Commentary on the Book of Isaiah I-XXVII* (ICC; T. & T. Clark: Edinburgh 1912) 141. See too J.D.W. Watts, *Isaiah 1-33* (WBC 24; Word Books: Waco 1985) 105; E.J. Young, *The Book of Isaiah.* The English Text, with Introduction, Exposition, and Notes. Vol. 1. Chapters 1-18 (Eerdmans: Grand Rapids ²1972) 29; H. Wildberger, *Jesaja.* 1. Teilband. Jesaja 1-12. (BKAT 10/1; Neukirchener Verlag: Neukirchen-Vluyn 1972) 302. On the governed noun in a construct phrase acting as subject, cf. Joüon - Muraoka, *Grammar*, #150n.

[8] For this understanding of הַשְּׂכִירָה, see Wildberger, *Jesaja* 1-12, 302 who does not, however, render the term at all in his translation. תִּסְפֶּה is given a masculine subject without explanation: 'und auch den Bart nimmt er weg'.

[9] Compare 'Janus' parallelism. Cf. G. Rendsburg, 'Double Polysemy in Genesis 49:6 and Job 3:6,' *CBQ* 44 (1982) 48-51; id., 'Notes on Genesis xv,' *VT* 42 (1992) 266-72: 266-268.

[10] Dahood, *Or* n.s. 48 (1979) 99.

and briers rather than the soil to 'grow up' and so Dahood makes קוֹץ שָׁמִיר the subject. The singular number of the verb does not create any difficulty since it can agree with one of the subjects.[11] The matter of gender is less easy since both nouns are masculine while the verb is apparently feminine. Dahood's answer is to parse תַּעֲלֶה as a masculine form. Traditional grammar suggests a different solution. Observing that קוֹץ שָׁמִיר are both translated by plural words, it is apparent that they must be considered as collectives after which a feminine verb is possible, although the instances of this phenomenon in Biblical Hebrew are 'fairly rare'.[12] Dahood's translation can be accepted, but it is unnecessary to posit the existence of masculine **taqtul*.[13]

לֹא־יִהְיֶה שָׁם אַרְיֵה
וּפְרִיץ חַיּוֹת בַּל־יַעֲלֶנָּה
לֹא תִמָּצֵא שָׁם
וְהָלְכוּ גְּאוּלִים (Isa 35,9)

No lion shall be there,
nor shall any ravenous beast come up on it;
they shall not be found there,
but the redeemed shall walk there. (RSV)

The lion shall not be there,
the fiercest of the beasts shall not come up it,

---

[11] Cf. Joüon - Muraoka, *Grammar*, #150q.

[12] Cf. Joüon - Muraoka, *Grammar*, #150e.

[13] Another analysis understands קוֹץ שָׁמִיר תַּעֲלֶה as a relative clause without morphological indicator, the antecedent of תַּעֲלֶה being אַדְמַת עַמִּי, while קוֹץ שָׁמִיר are accusatives of material placed before the verb: 'Over the land of my people, Coming up thorn and briar, ay, over all the pleasant houses, the whole merry city'. Cf. W.H. Irwin, *Isaiah 28-33:* Translation with Philological Notes (BibOr 30; Biblical Institute Press: Rome 1977) 130.

he shall not reach (תִמְצָא for MT תִּמָּצֵא) there. (Dahood)[14]

The question concerns the subject of תִּמָּצֵא. Dahood points out that if תִּמָּצֵא is third person feminine singular imperfect then it will require a feminine subject. אַרְיֵה and פְּרִיץ are both masculine and חַיּוֹת though feminine is plural, so that it too could not fulfil this function. *1QIsa*[a] reads ימצא, apparently taking אַרְיֵה as the subject.[15] Nevertheless, the MT may be retained. The practice of employing verbs in the feminine singular with plural animal names conceived as collectives is well attested and this could be an example.[16] In other words, אַרְיֵה conceived as a collective will be the subject of תִּמָּצֵא. It may be objected that אַרְיֵה is already the subject of a masculine form, יִהְיֶה, and that פְּרִיץ חַיּוֹת in the same way determines the gender of יַעֲלֶנָּה. Yet there is a further possibility, namely that the subject of תִּמָּצֵא is חַיּוֹת. חַיּוֹת is the governed noun in a construct chain and as such may be subject of a verb.[17] In that case חַיּוֹת will function as the subject of תִּמָּצֵא, as פְּרִיץ does of יַעֲלֶנָּה. The author would be making use of his liberty to employ as a subject first the governing noun in a construct chain and then the governed noun. This same freedom is not necessarily available to the translator who is governed by the rules of another language. The *waw* of וּפְרִיץ could be interpreted as emphatic or explicative:[18]

---

[14] Dahood, *Or* n.s. 48 (1979) 99-100.

[15] Cf. M. Burrows, *The Dead Sea Scrolls of St. Mark's Monastery* (ASOR: New Haven 1950) pl. xxviii.

[16] See Joüon - Muraoka, *Grammar*, #150g; *GKC*, #145k.

[17] Cf. Joüon - Muraoka, *Grammar*, #150n.

[18] For these functions of *waw*, consult *WOC*, #39.2.4; see also P. Wilton, 'More cases of *waw explicativum*,' *VT* 44 (1994) 125-128; Hans-Peter Müller, 'Nicht-junktiver Gebrauch von *w*- im Althebräischen,' *ZAH* 7 (1994) 141-174, esp. 147-156.

No lion shall be there,
the most ferocious of beasts[19] shall not come up
on it,
it shall not be found there.

תִּמָּצֵא may therefore be explained without postulating the existence of **taqtul*.

כָּאֲרִי כֵּן יְשַׁבֵּר כָּל־עַצְמוֹתָי
מִיּוֹם עַד־לַיְלָה תַּשְׁלִימֵנִי (Isa 38,13)
Like a lion he breaks all my bones;
from day to night thou dost bring me to an end. (RSV)

Like a lion, thus he breaks all my bones,
from morning till night he deprives me
of wholeness. (Dahood)[20]

The abrupt change of person from third to second in colon 2 of this verse Dahood finds unacceptable. On the other hand v. 14 features an imperative addressed to the Lord, which would lend some support to the second person in v. 13.[21] Furthermore, such switches are typical of West Semitic rhetoric in which changes of person do not necessarily imply changes of referent.[22]

Dahood parses תַּשְׁלִימֵנִי as a **taqtul* hiphil privative, pointing to the balance between יְשַׁבֵּר and תַּשְׁלִימֵנִי in support of his translation.

---

[19] Understanding פְּרִיץ חַיּוֹת as an instance of the superlative genitive. For examples, see conveniently, *WOC*, #9.5.3j (p. 154).

[20] Dahood, *Or* n.s. 48 (1979) 100.

[21] Cf. Schoors, '*Taqtul*', 196.

[22] Cf. S. Gevirtz, 'On Canaanite Rhetoric: The Evidence of the Amarna Letters from Tyre', *Or* n.s. 42 (1973) 162-177, esp. 170-171. See also Wildberger, *Jesaja* 2, 1443 n.b.

The hiphil privative is, however, at best a very rare phenomenon. G. Bergsträsser finds an instance in הוֹרִישׁ, hiphil of the verb ירשׁ which is denominative from יְרֻשָּׁה, 'property'. הוֹרִישׁ would then have the sense, 'taking away the property'.[23] Nevertheless, N. Lohfink has argued that the hiphil of ירשׁ needs to be distinguished. On the one hand it is present in early texts, not influenced by the deuteronomistic writers. In these texts (which are all poetic) the hiphil bears the sense 'make poor'. This suggests that semantically תַּשְׁלִימֵנִי should be linked with the hiphil of רושׁ rather than ירשׁ.[24] On the other hand in the deuteronomistic texts, although not limited to these, the hiphil of ירשׁ carries the sense of 'destroying'. In some cases this meaning is close to 'making poor' so that the semantic connection with רושׁ remains. In other texts the sense is rather of destroying with a view to taking over property, especially in the deuteronomistic passages.[25] It can be seen that the hiphil of ירשׁ can be explained without recourse to a hiphil privative whose existence has still to be demonstrated.

> רָאוֹת (ketib ראית) רַבּוֹת וְלֹא תִשְׁמֹר
> פָּקוֹחַ אָזְנַיִם וְלֹא יִשְׁמָע (Isa 42,20)
> He sees many things, but does not observe them;
> his ears are open, but he does not hear. (RSV)
>
> You see many things without taking note,
> your ears are open, but without hearing. (NAB)

---

[23] Cf. G. Bergsträsser, *Hebräische Grammatik* II. Teil: Verbum (Olms: Hildesheim 1962 [1929]) 104, #19g.

[24] Cf. N. Lohfink, 'Die Bedeutung von hebr. *jrš qal* und *hif*', *BZ* N.F. 27 (1983) 14-33, esp. 25-26. For a shorter version of this article, consult id., 'יָרַשׁ jāraš', *TWAT* III, 953-985 (*TDOT* VI, 368-396).

[25] Lohfink, 'Die Bedeutung', *BZ* N.F. 27 (1983) 26-32.

The RSV and NAB employ different persons, which points up the difficulty caused by the apparently incongruous parallel of תִשְׁמֹר and יִשְׁמָע. Some like the RSV would read both verbs as third person and emend תִשְׁמֹר to יִשְׁמֹר.[26] Nevertheless, the testimony of the ancient versions unanimously supports the MT.[27] Most modern commentators prefer to alter יִשְׁמָע to תִשְׁמָע, and so have both verbs in the second person.[28] This emendation finds some support in the ancient versions, for the second person plural is read in the LXX, Syriac and Targum, the second person singular in the Vulgate. While this solution has an obvious attraction it lacks support in the wider context.

Van Dijk observes that vv. 18, 19 and 21 make clear that the Servant is not being addressed.[29] V. 18 is an address to others, 'Hear you deaf and look you blind that you may see'. V. 19 continues in the third person, 'Who is blind but my servant...' Vv. 21-22 continue with the third person and v. 23 returns to the second person plural, 'Who among you will give ear to this...' Van Dijk therefore reads the third person throughout the verse.[30] Some prefer to follow the ketib, vocalised רָאִיתָ and therefore second person.[31] This would explain the form תִשְׁמֹר in the first stich, but then the third person in

---

[26] So for instance K. Elliger, *Deuterojesaja*. 1. Teilband *Jesaja 40,1- 45,7* (BK 11/1; Neukirchener Verlag: Neukirchen-Vluyn 1978) 272.

[27] Including *1QIsa*[a] which probably took it as second person because it also reads ראיתה, cf. Burrows, *Scrolls*, pl. xxxvi.

[28] See for instance J.L. McKenzie, *Second Isaiah*. Introduction, Translation, and Notes (AB 20; Doubleday: Garden City 1968) 45: the second person is required by the sense.

[29] Van Dijk, *VT* 19 (1969) 442. Elliger points out that a second person singular here clashes with the second person plural address in v. 18. Cf. Elliger, *Deuterojesaja*, 272.

[30] See too Elliger, *Deuterojesaja*, 272 n.b who emends to the third person יִשְׁמֹר.

[31] A. Schoors, *I am God Your Saviour*. A Form-Critical Study of the Main Genres in Is. XV-LV (VTS 24; Brill: Leiden 1973) 201; id., '*Taqtul*,' 199 n. 20.

the second stich is anomalous, and so יִשְׁמַע is altered to תִּשְׁמַע. One can point to *1QIsa*ª ראיתה for the vocalisation of the ketib. On the other hand van Dijk notes that the ketib can also be vocalised רָאִית and parsed as the infinitive absolute with the final *yod* of the root preserved.[32] In that case it would not show whether second or third person is intended.

The West Semitic penchant for abrupt changes of person even within a sentence or unit of thought has already been noted. It is probable that here too the text is intact and the change of person intended. The existence of **taqtul* cannot be deduced from this verse.

אִם־תָּשִׂים אָשָׁם נַפְשׁוֹ
יִרְאֶה זֶרַע יַאֲרִיךְ יָמִים (Isa 53,10bc)
When he makes himself an offering for sin,
he shall see his offspring,
he shall prolong his days. (RSV)

Van Dijk translates similarly, 'When he makes his life an offering for sin', commenting that this rendering is in accordance with that of the Vulgate, *si posuerit pro peccato animam suam*, and that the pronominal suffix in נַפְשׁוֹ can only be related to תָּשִׂים which must

[32] Van Dijk, '*Taqtul*,' 442 and n.3. The view is widely held that forms which show a final strong *waw* or *yod* are late developments, e.g. שָׁלַוְתִּי 'I was quiet' (Job 3,26) is judged to be late and denominative from שָׁלֵוָה 'quiet', see *BL*, #57t" (p. 426). In Ugaritic there is evidence for comparable forms with and without *waw* or *yod* coexisting, consult S. Segert, *A Basic Grammar of the Ugaritic Language: With Selected Texts and Glossary* (University of California Press: Berkeley 1984) #54.57 (pp. 74-75). In view of this, it appears likely that in Biblical Hebrew too some examples of a final strong *waw* or *yod* reflect an earlier tradition. See too R. Meyer, *Hebräische Grammatik* II: Formenlehre Flexionstabellen (De Gruyter: Berlin ³1966) #82c (p. 157).

then be masculine.[33] As van Dijk observes, to take נַפְשׁוֹ as the subject is difficult, and the text is frequently emended.[34] Nonetheless, *1QIsa*[a] reads תשים, which suggests that it is possible to make sense of the received text.[35] The RV in fact translates the verse

> Yet it pleased the LORD to bruise him;
> he hath put *him* to grief:
> when thou[36] shalt make his soul an offering for
> sin,
> he shall see *his* seed, he shall prolong *his* days,
> and the pleasure of the LORD shall prosper
> in his hand.

The unexpected change of person is no more strange than in the previous examples of alleged **taqtul* that have been considered. The prophet is reflecting on the fate of the Servant and then turns to address him who is responsible for it. In the last stich the third person indicates a return to reflection. Once again, there is no need to postulate a third person **taqtul*.

> וְאַתֶּם קִרְבוּ־הֵנָּה בְּנֵי עֹנְנָה
> זֶרַע מְנָאֵף וַתִּזְנֶה (Isa 57,3)
> But you, draw near hither, sons of the sorceress,
> offspring of the adulterer and the harlot. (RSV)

---

[33] Van Dijk, *VT* 19 (1979) 442-443. Dahood offers a new interpretation of the verse while agreeing with van Dijk that תָּשִׂים is masculine, but since there are other difficult points in his treatment it will not be considered here. Cf. Dahood, *Or* n.s. 48 (1979) 100.

[34] *BHK*[3] for instance suggests יָשִׂים, *BHS* תֻּשַּׂם.

[35] Cf. Burrows, *Scrolls*, pl. xliv.

[36] The NRSV also accepts the second person.

The difficulty lies in identifying the precise function of וַתִּזְנֶה. The RSV translates with a noun, following the LXX which renders *σπέρμα μοιχῶν καὶ πόρνης*, 'Seed of adulterers and a harlot,' and the Vulgate and Syriac.[37] At the same time *1QIsa*[a] reads ותזנו 'and you commit fornication', lending support to the MT.[38] Dahood translates the second stich, 'an adulterous and fornicating offspring', taking זֶרַע as the subject of וַתִּזְנֶה which he parses as masculine.[39] On the other hand Delitzsch retains the MT and translates, '(Kinder der Zauberin,) des Ehebrechers und einer Hurerischen Same'. He explains וַתִּזְנֶה as a relative clause, 'und (folglich) einer hurerisch sich Preisgebenden'.[40] This is a plausible view. In biblical poetry ellipsis of the relative pronoun is not uncommon and the only difficulty with וַתִּזְנֶה is the lack of an appropriate antecedent.[41] The translators of the LXX and the Vulgate employed a noun in place of the verb, understanding וַתִּזְנֶה as standing parallel to מְנָאֵף. The two words are in fact parallel, even though one is a noun and the other a verb. D. Grossberg points out the rhetorical value of the verb form in this verse

> The prophet heaps three abusive epithets on his people. The sudden appearance of the third in this imperfect verb form in place of the more common noun form is startling and infinitely more condemning than the more usual substantive, זונה 'whore', albeit a forceful one, would be. The partners in the adulterous relations, are the מנאף

[37] So too McKenzie, *Second Isaiah*, 156; *BHK*[3]; *BHS*.

[38] Burrows, *Scrolls*, pl. xlvii, followed by J.D.W. Watts, *Isaiah 34-66* (WBC 25; Word Books: Waco 1987) 254.

[39] Dahood, *Or* n.s. 48 (1979) 100-101.

[40] Cf. F. Delitzsch, *Commentar über das Buch Jesaia* (Leipzig 1889) 551.

[41] On the ellipsis of the relative pronoun, consult Joüon - Muraoka, *Grammar*, #129q, #158d.

> 'adulterer' and ותזנה 'she whored'. These two are governed by the construct זרע 'offspring (of)' and are counter-parts to בני ענגה 'children of a sorceress' in the parallel colon. They are, therefore, to be seen as a compound genitival unit, the finite form of one member of this compound notwithstanding.[42]

The translator may elect to employ a noun for the verb, but the verb form in the Hebrew is effective and conforms to the known grammar of the language. There is consequently no masculine **taqtul* present.

> גַּם־בְּנֵי־נֹף ותחפנס[43] יִרְעוּךְ קָדְקֹד׃
> הֲלוֹא־זֹאת תַּעֲשֶׂה־לָּךְ עָזְבֵךְ אֶת־יְהוָה אֱלֹהַיִךְ
> בְּעֵת מוֹלִיכֵךְ בַּדָּרֶךְ (Jer 2,16-17)
>
> Moreover, the men of Memphis and Tah'panhes have broken the crown of your head. Have you not brought this upon yourself by forsaking the LORD your God, when he led you in the way? (RSV)
>
> v.17: Don't you know what's really responsible—that you abandoned Yahweh your God... (Holladay)[44]
>
> v.17: Does not your forsaking of Yahweh, your God, bring this on you? (McKane)[45]

---

[42] Cf. D. Grossberg, 'Noun Verb Parallelism: Syntactic or Asyntactic?', *JBL* 99 (1980) 481-488, on 483.

[43] Qere תחפנחס.

[44] Cf. W.L. Holladay, *Jeremiah*. A Commentary on the Book of the Prophet Jeremiah Chapters 1-25 (Hermeneia; Fortress: Philadelphia 1986) 51.

[45] Cf. W. McKane, *A Critical and Exegetical Commentary on Jeremiah*. Introduction and Commentary on Jeremiah I- XXV (ICC; T. & T. Clark: Edinburgh 1986) 35. McKane deletes the last three words.

v.17: Behold, this have they done to you. (Dahood)[46]

The syntax of v. 17 is explained in different ways. Holladay (following the LXX) sees זאת as the subject of תַּעֲשֶׂה, the literal translation being 'Isn't this what is working on you? (namely)'? McKane on the other hand (following the Vulgate and Rashi) makes עָזְבֵךְ אֶת־יְהוָה אֱלֹהַיִךְ the subject, commenting that 'According to Duhm this grammar...necessitates the emendation of תַּעֲשֶׂה to יַעֲשֶׂה'.[47] The RSV also seems to understand the syntax in this way. The emendation is unnecessary. Although the infinitive is usually treated as masculine it can govern a feminine verb.[48] Dahood takes בְּנֵי־נֹף ותחפנס in v. 16 to be the subject of תַּעֲשֶׂה. This yields good sense, but there is no need to postulate **taqtul*. The subject can be understood as collective in which case the verb may be feminine singular.[49]

כִּי אֲנִי יְהוָה אֲדַבֵּר אֵת אֲשֶׁר אֲדַבֵּר דָּבָר וְיֵעָשֶׂה
לֹא תִמָּשֵׁךְ עוֹד כִּי בִימֵיכֶם בֵּית הַמֶּרִי אֲדַבֵּר דָּבָר וַעֲשִׂיתִיו
נְאֻם אֲדֹנָי יְהוִה (Ezek 12,25)

But I the LORD will speak the word
which I will speak, and it will be performed.
It will no longer be delayed, but in your days,
O rebellious house, I will speak the word and perform it, says the Lord GOD. (RSV)

For I Yahweh will speak what word I will speak, it will be done, it will not longer be delayed... (Van Dijk)[50]

---

46 M. Dahood, 'Hebrew-Ugaritic Lexicography X,' *Bib* 53 (1972) 392.
47 McKane, *Jeremiah* I, 38.
48 Consult *WOC*, #6.4.2e.
49 Cf. Joüon - Muraoka, *Grammar*, #150g.
50 Van Dijk, *VT* 19 (1969) 443.

דָּבָר is the subject of the two verbs יֵעָשֶׂה and תִּמָּשֵׁךְ, one of which is masculine, the other feminine. Commentators generally explain תִּמָּשֵׁךְ as third person feminine singular, expressing the neuter.[51] While this type of neuter is well attested in Biblical Hebrew, its use here is open to question. The preceding verb is masculine harmonizing with the masculine gender of דָּבָר. It is difficult to see why almost immediately afterwards the verb should be feminine. Brownlee recognises the inconsistency and emends to אמשך on the grounds that the MT 'has an unusual fem neuter subject'.[52] Van Dijk argues that 'the tightly interlocking structure' of וְיֵעָשֶׂה לֹא תִמָּשֵׁךְ precludes explaining תִּמָּשֵׁךְ as neuter and that תִּמָּשֵׁךְ is in fact masculine.[53] Relevant to the discussion is v. 28

> לָכֵן אֱמֹר אֲלֵיהֶם כֹּה אָמַר אֲדֹנָי יְהוִה
> לֹא־תִמָּשֵׁךְ עוֹד כָּל־דְּבָרָי אֲשֶׁר אֲדַבֵּר דָּבָר וְיֵעָשֶׂה
> נְאֻם אֲדֹנָי יְהוִה (Ezek 12,28)
> Therefore say to them, Thus says the Lord GOD:
> None of my words will be delayed any longer,
> but the word which I speak will be performed,
> says the Lord GOD. (RSV)

It can be seen that v. 28 repeats most of v. 25 but there is an interesting grammatical difference. In place of דָּבָר v. 28 reads

---

[51] Cf. G.A. Cooke, *A Critical and Exegetical Commentary on the Book of Ezekiel* (ICC; T. & T. Clark: Edinburgh 1936) 137; W. Zimmerli, *Ezechiel*. 1. Teilband. *Ezechiel 1-24* (BK 13/1; Neukirchener Verlag: Neukirchen-Vluyn 1969) 280 n.b (E.V. 275 n.b); M. Greenberg, *Ezekiel 1- 20.* A New Translation with Introduction and Commentary (AB 22; Doubleday: Garden City 1983) 229; Schoors, '*Taqtul*', 195.

[52] W.H. Brownlee, *Ezekiel 1-19* (WBC 28; Word: Waco 1986) 183.

[53] Van Dijk, *VT* 19 (1969) 444.

כָּל־דְּבָרַי preceded by the same verb that is problematic in v. 25, namely תִּמָּשֵׁךְ. The grammar in v. 28 is not problematic for a plural noun treated as a collective may take a feminine singular verb which then usually precedes the subject, as in v. 28, although this is not necessarily the case.[54] דָּבָר in v. 25 is singular in form but may nonetheless be a collective as often in Biblical Hebrew. Translations like ‘speech’, ‘edict’, ‘message’, ‘advice’, ‘request’, ‘promise’, ‘complaint’ and ‘sentence’ reflect this. Collective nouns may govern singular or plural verbs, but sometimes they also govern a feminine singular verb. This feature is found with names of peoples which are normally masculine. Here again the verb usually but not always comes first. Furthermore, the verb may alternate in number in adjacent passages. Joüon refers to Judg 9,36-37: הִנֵּה־עָם יוֹרְדִים...הִנֵּה־עָם יוֹרֵד where the same subject, albeit repeated, determines singular and plural verbs.[55] Ezek 12,25.28 while not themselves adjacent are in adjacent units. It would appear then that the author of Ezekiel is employing grammatical practices in an unusual but not impossible way. As a poet he feels free to stretch the standard grammar of prose and so he treats דָּבָר as a collective governing first a masculine and then a feminine verb. Muraoka draws attention to ‘the extraordinary vacillation’ of number in several passages of Ezekiel, and 12,25 illustrates this phenomenon.[56]

2. Minor Prophets and Psalms

אֶפְרַיִם לְשַׁמָּה תִהְיֶה בְּיוֹם תּוֹכֵחָה
בְּשִׁבְטֵי יִשְׂרָאֵל הוֹדַעְתִּי נֶאֱמָנָה (Hos 5,9)
Ephraim shall become a desolation in the day

[54] Cf. Joüon - Muraoka, *Grammar*, #150b,e.
[55] Cf. Joüon - Muraoka, *Grammar*, #150e. Also see 2 Sam 19,42-43.
[56] Ezek 1,5-26; 34,2-31; 37,1-11, cf. Joüon - Muraoka, *Grammar*, #150b, n.1.

of punishment;
among the tribes of Israel I declare what is sure. (RSV)

Ephraim shall become a ruin on the day of
punishment. (Dahood)[57]

The verb תִּהְיֶה if parsed as third person would be feminine, and yet its subject אֶפְרַיִם is invariably masculine.[58] Dahood therefore parses the verb as third person masculine. Nevertheless, names of peoples sometimes govern feminine verbs which usually but not always precede the subject.[59] In view of the immediately preceding vocative 'Benjamin', Andersen and Freedman parse the verb as second person masculine.[60] There is no need to suppose the existence of third person masculine **taqtul*.

וַתַּעֲשֶׂה אָדָם כִּדְגֵי הַיָּם
כְּרֶמֶשׂ לֹא־מֹשֵׁל בּוֹ (Hab 1,14)

For thou makest men like the fish of the sea,
like crawling things that have no ruler. (RSV)

For he gathers men like the fish of the sea,
like crawling things that have no ruler. (Van Dijk)[61]

Here the difficulty does not lie so much in an abrupt change of person as in the sense. Van Dijk points out that the verse is generally

[57] Cf. Dahood, *Or* n.s. 48 (1979) 101.

[58] This incongruity often goes unmentioned by commentators, cf. Harper, *Amos and Hosea*, 278; H.W. Wolff, *Dodekapropheton I: Hosea* (BKAT 14/1; Neukirchener Verlag: Neukirchen-Vluyn ^{2}1965) 131 (E.V. 104); D. Stuart, *Hosea-Jonah* (WBC 31; Word Books: Waco 1987) 97.

[59] Cf. Joüon - Muraoka, *Grammar*, #150e.

[60] Cf. F.I. Andersen and D.N. Freedman, *Hosea*. Introduction, Translation, and Notes (AB 24; Doubleday: Garden City 1980) 399.

[61] Van Dijk, *VT* 19 (1969) 446.

interpreted to mean that God treats men no better than the lower animals.[62] R.L. Smith argues that Habakkuk is comparing Babylon's treatment of captives to a fisherman's treatment of fish, but God has appointed her to do it (see v. 12).[63] This does not harmonise with God's interest in the faithfulness of man expressed in v. 13, or with his joy at gathering men in v. 15. Van Dijk tries to resolve the difficulty by parsing וַתַּעֲשֶׂה as third person masculine, with the nuance 'gather'. Traditional grammar recognises, however, that a plural subject when viewed as a collective may govern a singular feminine verb which usually though not invariably precedes the subject.[64] Here the subject would be 'the wicked' of the preceding verse who do treat men like the lower animals. Hence, one may render

For they make men like the fish of the sea,
like crawling things that have no ruler.

The meaning of v. 14 is discussed, but even if van Dijk's argumentation is accepted and the verb parsed as third person, it is not necessary to postulate the existence of masculine **taqtul*.

וְנֹגַהּ כָּאוֹר תִּהְיֶה קַרְנַיִם מִיָּדוֹ לוֹ
וְשָׁם חֶבְיוֹן עֻזֹּה (Hab 3,4)
His brightness was like the light,
rays flashed from his hand;
and there he veiled his power. (RSV)

[62] So for example Ward in J.M.P. Smith, W.H. Ward, J.A. Bewer, *A Critical and Exegetical Commentary on Micah, Zephaniah, Nahum, Habakkuk. Obadiah and Joel* (ICC; T. & T. Clark: Edinburgh 1912) 11.

[63] Cf. R.L. Smith, *Micah-Malachi* (WBC 32; Word Books: Waco 1984) 104.

[64] Cf. Joüon - Muraoka, *Grammar*, #150e; *GKC*, #145k.

Dahood asserts that נֹגַה is masculine in form and that תִּהְיֶה must then be masculine.[65] It is true that the verb is often emended. *BHK*[3] requires a change to יִהְיֶה or תַּחְתָּיו, *BHS* simply to תַּחְתָּיו. Yet form is no sure guide to gender.[66] It remains quite possible that נֹגַה is feminine. There is consequently no sufficient reason for emending the text or for assuming the existence of **taqtul*.[67]

יִגְמָר־נָא רַע רְשָׁעִים
וּתְכוֹנֵן צַדִּיק
וּבֹחֵן לִבּוֹת וּכְלָיוֹת
אֱלֹהִים צַדִּיק (Ps 7,10)

O let the evil of the wicked come to an end,
but establish thou the righteous,
thou who triest the minds and hearts,
thou righteous God. (RSV)

May he avenge the evil of the wicked,
and reassure the just man;
since searcher of minds and hearts
is God the Just. (Dahood)[68]

Dahood argues as follows

> Ps 7 appears to be divided into two strophes, the first, vss. 2-9, addressing God directly in the second person,

[65] Dahood, *Or* n.s. 48 (1979) 101.

[66] Cf. D. Michel, *Grundlegung einer hebräischen Syntax* Teil I: *Sprachwissenschaftliche Methodik Genus und Numerus des Nomens* (Neukirchener Verlag: Neukirchen-Vluyn 1977) 68-79.

[67] No emendation of תִּהְיֶה is suggested by Smith, *Micah-Malachi*, 114; J. Tuillén Torralba, 'Yahvé, mi salvador: Habacuc, 3', *Isidorianum* 10 (1996) 95-123, on 102.

[68] Dahood, *Or* n.s. 48 (1979) 101-102.

> while the second strophe, vss. 10-18, speaks of God in the third person. Hence when paired with third-person *yigmornā'*, *t^ekônēn* readily parses as 3rd masc. sg. employed here for stylistic variation.

It is true that there is an alternation of person in the psalm and that this is connected with the structure. Nevertheless, in view of the West Semitic practice of abrupt alternation of person, it seems unsafe to make person the criterion for establishing the structure of the psalm. Dahood takes the first 'strophe' to be vv. 2-9, but other scholars make different divisions. There seems to be no further difficulty and the commentators do not allude to this alternation of person.[69] It seems best to keep the traditional understanding of תְּכוֹנֵן as second person.

> עַל־מֶה נִאֵץ רָשָׁע אֱלֹהִים
> אָמַר בְּלִבּוֹ לֹא תִּדְרֹשׁ (Ps 10,13)
> Why does the wicked renounce God,
> and say in his heart, 'Thou wilt not call to account'? (RSV)
>
> The wicked despises God for ever,[70]
> he says in his heart, 'He does not requite'. (Van Dijk)

Since the wicked despises God, it seems strange that he should trouble to address him. For this reason ancient and modern translators generally read the second person תִּדְרֹשׁ, which also harmonises with

[69] See, for instance, G. Ravasi, *Il Libro dei Salmi*. Commento e attualizzazione. Vol. 1 (Testi et commenti 1; Dehoniane: Bologna 1985) 166: 'rendi stabile il giusto,' without a note.

[70] Reading עָלְמָה for MT עַל־מֶה. Cf. van Dijk, *VT* 19 (1969) 446.

vv. 3-4.[71] Ravasi observes that the MT is odd and draws attention to the versions. He explains the MT as 'perhaps' **taqtul*.[72] Nevertheless, van Dijk points out that the MT is possible in itself, though he prefers the third person for stylistic reasons. There is certainly a lack of logic in the evildoer addressing the God whom he despises, but no doubt in the mind of the psalmist the wicked lack logic. The reader is being shown the futility of the would-be agnostic's attempt to distance himself from God. It is accordingly no accident that the address jarrs. The second person should be retained.

יְהוָה יִשְׁמְרֵהוּ וִיחַיֵּהוּ
יאשר [ואשר] בָּאָרֶץ
וְאַל־תִּתְּנֵהוּ בְּנֶפֶשׁ אֹיְבָיו׃
יְהוָה יִסְעָדֶנּוּ עַל־עֶרֶשׂ דְּוָי
כָּל־מִשְׁכָּבוֹ הָפַכְתָּ בְחָלְיוֹ (Ps 41,3-4)[73]

The LORD protects him and keeps him alive;
he is called blessed in the land;
thou dost not give him up to the will of his enemies.
(v.4) The LORD sustains him on his sickbed;
in his illness thou healest all his infirmities. (RSV)

May Yahweh protect him and grant him long life,
may he be rendered happy upon earth,
and may He not put him into the maw of his Foe. (Dahood)[74]

---

[71] See the LXX, Vulgate and Syriac. Some commentators experience no difficulty. There is not even a reference to the reading of the versions in H.-J. Kraus, *Psalmen*. 1 Teilband *Psalmen 1-59* (BK 15/1; Neukirchener Verlag: Neukirchen-Vluyn [5]1978) 216, 217.

[72] Ravasi, *Salmi* 1, 207, 227 n.35.

[73] In v. 3 the qere is placed between square brackets.

[74] Dahood, *Or* n.s. 48 (1979) 102.

Here again the abrupt change of person exercises translators and commentators. The LXX, Vulgate and numerous moderns employ the third person throughout v. 3.[75] Dahood also accepts this view, explaining

> Often emended to *yitt^{e}nēhû* on the authority of some ancient versions, *titt^{e}nēhû* can stand as 3rd masc. sing. chosen here to provide some variation in the midst of five masculine singular forms with preformative *y*- in vss. 2-4.

The point about variation is well taken, but v. 4 suggests that the psalmist may not be intending to offer a third person with תִּתְּנֵהוּ. The translation of the second stich of v. 4 is discussed, but the second person is usually retained.[76] It seems clear that הָפַכְתָּ which is perfect and second person is parallel to the third person imperfect יִסְעָדֶנּוּ. In the same way, v. 3 alternates between third person and second person. It is therefore best to take also תִּתְּנֵהוּ in v. 3 as second person.[77]

כְּאַיָּל תַּעֲרֹג עַל־אֲפִיקֵי־מָיִם
כֵּן נַפְשִׁי תַעֲרֹג אֵלֶיךָ אֱלֹהִים (Ps 42,2)
As a hart longs for flowing streams,
so longs my soul for thee, O God. (RSV)

The grammatical difficulty lies in the lack of agreement between the apparently masculine subject אַיָּל and the feminine predicate תַּעֲרֹג.[78]

---

[75] For a convenient listing of authorities, see L. Alonso Schökel - C. Carniti, *Salmos* I (Verbo Divino: Estella 1992-1993) 603.

[76] An exception is Alonso - Carniti, *Salmos* I, 603.

[77] Cf. Ravasi, *Salmi* 1, 742 n.1.

[78] Van Dijk, *VT* 19 (1969) 444-445.

Some would read אַיֶּלֶת in the absolute state.[79] On the other hand, as van Dijk points out, this is found elsewhere only in Jer 14,15. He adds that 'its occurrence here would unduly impede the metre of the first colon' and concludes that a masculine **taqtul* 'could provide the best solution to explain the grammatical structure of this vs'. The two cola are in fact exactly equal in length with twelve syllables each and this may explain the shorter form. One may compare דֹּב, an epicene noun, to be rendered 'she-bear' in some passages.[80] אַיָּל is feminine despite the lack of a feminine ending. There is no need to postulate the existence of **taqtul*.[81]

> בְּרוּחַ קָדִים תְּשַׁבֵּר אֳנִיּוֹת תַּרְשִׁישׁ (Ps 48,8)
>
> By the east wind thou didst shatter the ships of Tarshish. (RSV)
>
> With the east wind he shattered the ships of Tarshish. (Dahood)[82]

Dahood argues that the psalm divides into two strophes: vv. 2-9 and 10-15. The first speaks of God in the third person, the second in the second person. Hence, תְּשַׁבֵּר which is in v. 8 and therefore in the first strophe should be third person. This is a popular option with commentators who in view of the parallelism with v. 7 further emend בְּרוּחַ to כְּרוּחַ:

---

[79] Schoors, '*Taqtul*', 195.

[80] Cf. *BDB*, 179a; A.B. Ehrlich, *Die Psalmen*. Neu übersetzt und erklärt (Berlin 1905) 95; Levi, *Inkongruenz*, 14-15; *WOC*, #6.5.2 (p. 107).

[81] See the comment of Ravasi, *Salmi* 1, 765 n.11.

[82] Dahood, *Or* n.s. 48 (1970) 102.

Like the east wind that shatters the ships of
Tarshish.[83]

The emendation is unnecessary because כ in the previous verse can extend its force to בְּרוּחַ:[84] 'As when by the east wind...' The change to the third person is also debatable. The LXX and Vulgate witness to the second person which may simply be a case of an abrupt change for rhetorical effect. In the second part of the psalm the second person is employed and the poet may wish to prepare for this towards the end of the first part. Hence, Dahood's proposal is not compelling.

כִּי לֹא בְמוֹתוֹ יִקַּח הַכֹּל
לֹא־יֵרֵד אַחֲרָיו כְּבוֹדוֹ׃
כִּי־נַפְשׁוֹ בְּחַיָּיו יְבָרֵךְ
וְיוֹדֻךָ כִּי־תֵיטִיב לָךְ׃
תָּבוֹא עַד־דּוֹר אֲבוֹתָיו
עַד־נֵצַח לֹא יִרְאוּ־אוֹר (Ps 49,18-20)

For when he dies he will carry nothing away;
his glory will not go down after him.
(v.19) Though, while he lives, he counts himself
happy,
and though a man gets praise when he does well
for himself,
(v.20) he will go to the generation of his fathers,
who will never more see the light. (RSV)

[83] P.C. Craigie, *Psalms 1-50* (WBC 19; Word Books: Waco 1983) 351. Cf. A.B. Ehrlich, *Die Psalmen*. Neu übersetzt und erklärt (Berlin 1905) 107; Kraus, *Psalmen* 1, 510 n.h; Ravasi, *Salmi* 1, 854, 863 n.12.

[84] See M. Dahood, *Psalms* I 1-50. Introduction, Translation, and Notes (AB 16; Doubleday: Garden City 1966) 291.

A glance at the Hebrew of vv. 19-20 shows that the translation of the RSV has smoothed over some difficulties. In particular, the Hebrew second person has been changed to third. For v. 19 this may not appear problematic, as English idiom permits the use of the third person with an impersonal subject. At the same time the second person is equally acceptable. In Hebrew it is normally the third person that is employed with an impersonal subject, but occasionally the second person masculine singular is found.[85] After the same manner, the RSV employs the third person for תָּבוֹא in v. 20, but now the matter is more difficult since the suffix on the verb's complement, אֲבוֹתָיו, is third person. To avoid this incongruity between verb and complement, some expressly emend תָּבוֹא to יָבוֹא.[86] Briggs and Briggs take the subject to be the soul or self which being feminine permits תָּבוֹא to function as third person.[87] The masculine suffix on אֲבוֹתָיו then refers back to אִישׁ (v. 17). Dahood proposes to parse תָּבוֹא as third person masculine singular. Others accept the second person.[88] Here again the West Semitic penchant for abrupt change of person helps to explain the bewildering alternation. The changes of person are stylistic, though this does not mean only formal. The direct address of the second person reminds the audience that they should take the psalmist's message to heart. Meanwhile, translators have to find an appropriate idiom in their own language. The MT should be retained.

יְאֶתָיו חַשְׁמַנִּים מִנִּי מִצְרָיִם

[85] Cf. *GKC*, #144h.

[86] Kraus, *Psalmen* I, 518 n.w; Craigie, *Psalms 1-50*, 357.

[87] C.A. Briggs - E.G. Briggs, *A Critical and Exegetical Commentary on the Book of Psalms* (T. & T. Clark: Edinburgh 1907) I, 412. Also see Schoors, '*Taqtul*', 197.

[88] Cf. Ehrlich, *Psalmen*, 111; Ravasi, *Salmi* 1, 892 n.33 (but see 870 n.4 where the third person is employed).

כּוּשׁ תָּרִיץ יָדָיו לֵאלֹהִים (Ps 68,32)

Let bronze be brought from Egypt;
let Ethiopia hasten to stretch out her hands to God. (RSV)

Kush speeds his wares to God. (Dahood)[89]

The word כּוּשׁ is normally masculine but here it governs the verb תָּרִיץ. Tate observes that the lack of agreement in gender may be 'anomalous'.[90] Briggs and Briggs however take כּוּשׁ as *casus pendens* and יָדָיו as the subject of the verb.[91] One might also understand כּוּשׁ as collective, representing a people, which can then govern a feminine singular verb. In any case, Dahood's suggestion to parse תָּרִיץ as masculine does not impose itself.

עָשָׂה יָרֵחַ לְמוֹעֲדִים
שֶׁמֶשׁ יָדַע מְבוֹאוֹ:
תָּשֶׁת־חֹשֶׁךְ וִיהִי לָיְלָה
בּוֹ־תִרְמֹשׂ כָּל־חַיְתוֹ־יָעַר (Ps 104,19-20)

Thou hast made the moon to mark the seasons;
the sun knows its time for setting.
(v.20) Thou makest darkness, and it is night,
when all the beasts of the forest creep forth. (RSV)

(v.20a) He settles darkness and night comes on. (Dahood)[92]

---

89 Dahood, *Or* n.s. 48 (1979) 103.

90 Tate, *Psalms 51-100*, 169, who refers to *GKC*, #146g. In the example there, however, the subject includes a feminine noun. On apparent anomalies in gender, cf. Levi, *Inkongruenz*.

91 Briggs - Briggs, *Psalms* II, 105 (see 112); so too Ehrlich, *Psalmen*, 157.

92 Dahood, *Or* n.s. 48 (1979) 103.

Vv. 19-20 are parallel, and the abrupt change of person in v. 20 jarrs. Even the normally conservative RSV feels constrained to smooth over the difficulty, offering a second person in v. 19 for the third person עָשָׂה of the MT. Dahood points out that in vv. 10-23 God is otherwise spoken of in the third person, and so he parses תָּשֶׁת as third person masculine. The alternation of person in the psalm may be considered more closely. In the opening verse the psalmist addresses God directly and this continues until v. 9. With v. 10 begins a passage speaking of God in the third person, but v. 24 resumes the direct address which is replaced by the third person in v. 31. V. 35b concludes the psalm with a partial repetition of the address in v. 1a. It is true that vv. 10-23 employ the third person in reference to God (v. 20 excepted), but in this section the only such third person indication after v. 20 is the mention of young lions seeking their food מֵאֵל in v. 21. V. 24 then brings a renewed address to the Lord. It looks then as if in v. 20 the psalmist is already preparing for a renewed address. The abrupt change in v. 20 is more immediately for rhetorical effect. Where v. 19 speaks tranquilly of God as the creator, v. 20 by addressing him turns reflection into prayer. This sudden alternation is striking but harmonises with the alternation of person in the psalm as a whole. Most commentators have no difficulty with the second person, but they usually understand it as volitive, 'Make darkness'.[93] In view of the alternation of person throughout the psalm it is also feasible to keep the indicative. There is no need to postulate **taqtul*.

---

[93] See Joüon - Muraoka, *Grammar*, #167a; Briggs - Briggs, *Psalms* I, 338; Ravasi, *Salmi* 3, 82 n.6. The indicative second person is favoured by H.-J. Kraus, *Psalmen* 2. Teilband: *Psalmen 60-150* (BKAT 15/2; Neukirchener Verlag: Neukirchen-Vluyn [5]1978) 878 and L.C. Allen, *Psalms 101-150* (WBC 21; Word Books: Waco 1983) 25.

תִּזְרַח הַשֶּׁמֶשׁ יֵאָסֵפוּן וְאֶל־מְעוֹנֹתָם יִרְבָּצוּן (Ps 104,22)
When the sun rises, they get them away and lie
down in their dens. (RSV)

Dahood argues that in v. 19 שֶׁמֶשׁ is treated as masculine (שֶׁמֶשׁ יָדַע מְבוֹאוֹ, 'the sun knows its setting') and presumably has the same gender in v. 22 so that תִּזְרַח is masculine.[94] He compares Gen 32,32, וַיִּזְרַח־לוֹ הַשֶּׁמֶשׁ, 'and the sun rose over him'. Nevertheless, שֶׁמֶשׁ sometimes governs a feminine verb, as in Gen 15,17 הַשֶּׁמֶשׁ בָּאָה, 'the sun went down'.[95] Dahood's argument is therefore not conclusive.

וַיֹּאמֶר וַיַּעֲמֵד רוּחַ סְעָרָה וַתְּרוֹמֵם גַּלָּיו (Ps 107,25)
For he commanded, and raised the stormy wind,
which lifted up the waves of the sea. (RSV)

He commanded and raised the wind, the storm,
and he lifted high its billows. (Dahood)[96]

For Dahood God is the subject of וַיֹּאמֶר and וַיַּעֲמֵד, and by parsing וַתְּרוֹמֵם as masculine he can keep him as the subject. The RSV represents the general opinion which takes רוּחַ as the subject of וַתְּרוֹמֵם. This is grammatically unexceptionable and makes good sense. Hence, there is no need to posit **taqtul* here.

[94] Dahood, *Or* n.s. 48 (1979) 103.

[95] Cf. K. Albrecht, 'Das Geschlecht der hebräischen Hauptwörter,' *ZAW* 15 (1895) 324; Michel, *Grundlegung*, 78. Not a few words in Biblical Hebrew are found with two genders, cf. Levi, *Inkongruenz*, 13.

[96] Dahood, *Or* n.s. 48 (1979) 103.

3. Job, Proverbs, Lamentations

עַיִן שְׁזָפַתּוּ וְלֹא תוֹסִיף   וְלֹא־עוֹד תְּשׁוּרֶנּוּ מְקוֹמוֹ (Job 20,9)
The eye which saw him will see him no more,
nor will his place any more behold him. (RSV)

The eye which glimpsed him shall do so no more,
and shall never again see him in his place. (NEB)

The apparently feminine form תְּשׁוּרֶנּוּ seems to imply that מְקוֹמוֹ its subject is feminine. Other passages where this noun appears to be feminine are Gen 18,24 and 2 Sam 17,12 (ketib).[97] In Gen 18,24 בְּקִרְבָּהּ is probably better repointed בְּקִרְבֹּה, which still leaves 2 Sam 17,12.[98] In Job the noun is otherwise always masculine. Sarna points out that a phrase equivalent to the second half of the verse appears in 7,10 and Ps 103,16: וְלֹא־יַכִּירֶנּוּ עוֹד מְקֹמוֹ, 'nor will his place know him any more'. Here מְקֹמוֹ is undoubtedly masculine and the subject of יַכִּירֶנּוּ. Sarna believes that in our verse too מְקֹמוֹ is masculine and and that תְּשׁוּרֶנּוּ must also be so. Van Dijk takes the same view.[99] Some like the NEB take עַיִן as the subject of תְּשׁוּרֶנּוּ, מְקוֹמוֹ then being an accusative. This is certainly grammatically possible.[100] Nonetheless, the parallelism is inferior and it appears a trifle awkward. The translation of the RSV looks better, but the assumption that מְקֹמוֹ is feminine requires an explanation.

---

[97] Cf. *GKC*, #122l.

[98] Cf. Albrecht, *ZAW* 16 (1896) 53; Levi, *Inkongruenz*, 13.

[99] Van Dijk, *VT* 19 (1969) 447; N. Sarna, 'The Mythological Background of Job 18,' *JBL* 82 (1963) 318.

[100] Cf. Schoors, '*Taqtul*', 194 and n.14.

Alonso Schökel emphasises the importance of reciting poetry aloud.[101] Reading this verse aloud one is struck by the repetition of initial consonants. The first three words of the second stich begin with the same consonants as three of the words in the first. The letter שׂ which begins שְׂזָפַתּוּ is not found opening a word in the second stich, but it is the first root consonant of the parallel verb תְּשׁוּרֶנּוּ. Leaving aside מְקֹמוֹ, there is a remarkable parallel between the initial sounds of the two stichs, and the preformative ת in תְּשׁוּרֶנּוּ forms part of the pattern. A preformative י would impair the symmetry. The poet then took the 'bold' step of treating מְקֹמוֹ as feminine in order to obtain an alliteration which binds the two stichs more closely together.[102] There is then no need either to emend the text or to postulate **taqtul*.

עַצְמוֹתָיו מָלְאוּ עלומו וְעִמּוֹ עַל־עָפָר תִּשְׁכָּב (Job 20,11)[103]
His bones are full of youthful vigor,
but it will lie down with him in the dust. (RSV)

This verse may provide another instance of a plural noun treated as a collective governing a singular verb. עֲלוּמִים* is treated as plural by the qere in accordance with its other occurrences and is followed by the singular verb תִּשְׁכָּב, even though עַצְמוֹתָיו governs the plural verb מָלְאוּ.[104]

[101] See for example L. Alonso Schökel, *A Manual of Hebrew Poetics* (Subsidia Biblica 11; Pontificio Istituto Biblico: Roma 1988) 20-33 [*Manual de poética hebrea* (Cristiandad: Madrid 1987) 38-52].

[102] It has been suggested that מְקֹמוֹ is dialectally feminine. Cf. W. Moran, '**taqtul* - Third Masculine Singular?' *Bib* 45 (1964) 82 n.1. This may well be the case, but it does not explain why the feminine gender was chosen in this particular verse.

[103] Qere עלומיו.

[104] The ketib does not necessarily imply the singular.

הַאַף שׂוֹנֵא מִשְׁפָּט יַחֲבוֹשׁ וְאִם־צַדִּיק כַּבִּיר תַּרְשִׁיעַ (Job 34,17)
Shall one who hates justice govern?
Will you condemn him who is righteous and mighty? (RSV)

Can an enemy of the (sic) right bind up,
or pronounce the Venerable Just One guilty? (Dahood)[105]

Dahood observes that the Targum and two manuscripts read the third person יַרְשִׁיעַ for תַּרְשִׁיעַ of the MT 'since there is no apparent motive for the shift of persons'.[106] Rather than emend the text, he understands תַּרְשִׁיעַ as masculine. Gray argues that starting with v. 16 Elihu is addressing Job directly.[107] In any case, the abrupt change of person is a rhetorical device to alert the hearer to the significance of the message. The verb תַּרְשִׁיעַ should therefore not be changed but rather understood as second person.

אַךְ־שָׁוְא לֹא־יִשְׁמַע אֵל וְשַׁדַּי לֹא יְשׁוּרֶנָּה׃
אַף כִּי־תֹאמַר לֹא תְשׁוּרֶנּוּ דִּין לְפָנָיו וּתְחוֹלֵל לוֹ (Job 35,13-14)
Surely God does not hear an empty cry,
nor does the Almighty regard it.
(v.14) How much less when you say that you do not see him, that the case is before him, and you are waiting for him! (RSV)

(v.14) Even though you say he does not look upon it,

---

[105] Dahood, *Or* n.s. 48 (1979) 104.

[106] The text may be emended accordingly, see G. Fohrer, *Das Buch Hiob* (KAT 16; Mohn: Gütersloh 1963) 464.

[107] S.R. Driver - G.B. Gray, *A Critical and Exegetical Commentary on the Book of Job together with a New Translation* (ICC; T. & T. Clark: Edinburgh 1921) I, 297-298.

the case is before him and so entreat
him. (Dahood)[108]

Dahood argues that since the verbs יִשְׁמַע and יְשׁוּרֶנָּה in v. 13 are predicated of El Shaddai, he should also be the subject of תְּשׁוּרֶנּוּ in v. 14, a position supported by the Vulgate and the Targum. Here again it is a matter of rhetorical technique. By making Job the subject of a verb which has just been predicated of God, Elihu subtly indicates that Job is trying to make himself the equal of El Shaddai. תְּשׁוּרֶנּוּ is not an instance of *taqtul*.

לֹא־יִשָּׂא פְּנֵי כָל־כֹּפֶר וְלֹא־יֹאבֶה כִּי תַרְבֶּה־שֹׁחַד (Prov 6,35)
He will accept no compensation,
nor be appeased though you multiply gifts. (RSV)

No payment whatever will placate him,
nor will he accept however large the bribe. (Dahood)[109]

Dahood argues that 'In vss. 32-35 which describe the behaviour of the adulterer and the reaction of the offended husband, there is no sign of a second-person verb or suffix'. Hence, he would parse תַרְבֶּה as a hiphil elative whose subject is the masculine שֹׁחַד. Both the LXX and the Vulgate take this verb as third person. Nevertheless, although this understanding of the text may be attractive, it is not the only possible one. V. 35 concludes chap. 6 which begins with the address, בְּנִי, 'my son,' and continues with בְּנִי in v. 20. There follow general remarks about the importance of keeping the law, and then from v. 24

[108] Dahood, *Or* n.s. 48 (1979) 105.

[109] Dahood, *Or* n.s. 48 (1979) 105. On the rendering 'him' in the first stich Dahood comments in n.29, 'Literally, "will lift up his face", with the suffix of *pny* analyzed as 3rd sing. *-y* as in Phoenician'. The matter is irrelevant to the issue of **taqtul*.

to the end of the chapter comes a disquisition on adultery. In vv. 24-25 the second person is employed, and it is therefore not inappropriate to find the second person again at the end of the pericope, eliciting an inclusion. Hence, תַּרְבֶּה may be understood as second person.

> מֵשִׁיב רָעָה תַּחַת טוֹבָה
> לֹא־תמיש[110] רָעָה מִבֵּיתוֹ (Prov 17,13)
> If a man returns evil for good,
> evil will not depart from his house. (RSV)
>
> One who returns evil for good will never remove
> trouble from his house. (Dahood)[111]

As Dahood points out, the qere (תָמוּשׁ) 'makes good syntax and sense' and is normally followed. He would explain the ketib as hiphil masculine singular dependent on the masculine subject of מֵשִׁיב. He adds that the hiphil may be used intransitively with the sense of 'depart' as in Ps 55,12. In either case the ketib can be followed. Dahood's version does keep the verse moving forward, but the existence of **taqtul* cannot be demonstrated from this verse.

> תִּקְרָא כְיוֹם מוֹעֵד מְגוּרַי מִסָּבִיב
> וְלֹא הָיָה בְּיוֹם אַף־יְהוָה פָּלִיט וְשָׂרִיד
> אֲשֶׁר־טִפַּחְתִּי וְרִבִּיתִי אֹיְבִי כִלָּם (Lam 2,22)
> Thou didst invite as to the day of an appointed
> feast my terrors on every side; and on the day of
> the anger of the LORD none escaped or survived;

---

110 Qere תמוש.

111 Dahood, *Or* n.s. 48 (1979) 105.

those whom I dandled and reared my enemy destroyed. (RSV)

(v.22a) He summoned the very day[112] of the assembly my assailants on every side. (Dahood)[113]

Dahood argues that תִּקְרָא should parse as third masculine singular since אַף־יְהוָה, 'Yahweh's wrath' is third person. He notes that Alexandrinus and Vaticanus render the verb by ἐκάλεσεν, 'He summoned'.[114] Yet the phrase יוֹם אַף־יְהוָה is a fixed expression with a clear meaning appropriate to the speaker's stress on the completeness of the disaster. That may be the explanation for the change of person. Hence, a third person verb is actually less consonant with the speaker's intentions. Commentators generally find no difficulty in taking the verb as second person.[115]

וַתִּזְנַח מִשָּׁלוֹם נַפְשִׁי נָשִׁיתִי טוֹבָה (Lam 3,17)
my soul is bereft of peace,
I have forgotten what happiness is. (RSV)

He spurned my peaceless soul,
I have forgotten what happiness is. (Dahood)[116]

Some like the RSV consider the subject of וַתִּזְנַח to be נַפְשִׁי, but the verb normally takes a direct object so that the preposition in מִשָּׁלוֹם

112 Reading כְּיוֹם for MT כְּיוֹם.

113 M. Dahood, 'New Readings in Lamentations,' *Bib* 59 (1978) 181-182; id., *Or* n.s. 48 (1979) 105-106.

114 Dahood, *Bib* 59 1978) 181.

115 Cf. D.R. Hillers, *Lamentations*. A New Translation with Introduction and Commentary (AB 7A; Doubleday: New York ^{2}1992) 96; H.-J. Kraus, *Klagelieder (Threni)* (BKAT 20; Neukirchener Verlag: Neukirchen-Vluyn 1956) 32.

116 Dahood, *Or* n.s. 48 (1979) 106.

requires explanation. Hummel transfers the initial מ to the preceding word, postulating an enclitic *mem*, וַתִּזְנַח-ם, which would solve the problem.[117] Another view is that if ותזנח were pointed as a niphal, the following *mem* would not cause difficulty.[118] The niphal of זנח is not, however, otherwise attested in the Hebrew Bible.[119] Dahood interprets the preposition as privative and makes נַפְשִׁי the object of the verb with Yahweh the subject. This rendering finds support from the LXX which translates *καὶ ἀπώσατο ἐξ εἰρήνης ψυχήν μου*, 'he has also removed my soul from peace'. Kraus understands the phrase similarly but takes וַתִּזְנַח to be second person, 'Du verstießest aus dem Wohlsein mein Leben'.[120] This is unexceptionable. While 'Yahweh' is the subject of third person verbs in the previous lines and is spoken of in the third person in the following line, such sudden changes of person are not uncommon as has already been noted. Here the abrupt switch focuses the reader's attention more sharply on the source of the speaker's misery. The second person may therefore be retained.

This consideration of possible cases of masculine **taqtul* has shown that the alleged instances of this form can be explained in other ways. The principal alternative explanations have been a deliberate change of person for rhetorical effect, and a subject understood as collective which may govern a feminine singular verb. Examples of a deliberate change of person could be Deut 32,14; Isa 38,13; 42,20; 53,10bc; Hos 5,9(?); Ps 7,10; 10,13; 41,3; 48,8; Job 34,17; Lam 2,22. A collective subject may be found in Isa 32,13; 35,9;

---

[117] H.D. Hummel, 'Enclitic *Mem* in Early Northwest Semitic, especially Hebrew,' *JBL* 76 (1957) 105. So too T.F. McDaniel, 'Philological Studies in Lamentations. II,' *Bib* 49 (1968) 201; Hillers, *Lamentations*, 114.

[118] So, for instance, J.A. Emerton, 'Are there examples of enclitic *mem* in the Hebrew Bible?', *Texts, Temples, and Traditions*. A tribute to Menahem Haran (ed. M.V. Fox et al.) (Eisenbrauns: Winona Lake 1996) 321-338:334.

[119] Cf. H. Ringgren, 'זָנַח *zānaḥ*', *TWAT* II, 619-621:619.

[120] Kraus, *Klagelieder*, 46, 47 n.k.

Hos 5,9(?); Hab 1,14; Ps 68,32. A few passages cannot be explained in either of these ways, and special explanations must be sought, which conform to known Hebrew grammar and yet allow the author to exercise a certain poetic licence. Examples of this would be Isa 57,3; Ezek 12,25; Job 20,9. At the same time, while it has not been possible to accept **taqtul*, the hypothesis of its existence has forced scholars to consider the received text more carefully and seek explanations of it without resorting to emendation. This will benefit exegesis.

4

Does Biblical Hebrew know a Third Person Singular Suffix in *-y*? A Reconsideration of the Evidence

1. The Book of Job

In 1962 Dahood suggested that final *yod* in Biblical Hebrew could represent the third person singular pronominal suffix, as it regularly does in standard Phoenician.[1] It was not in fact a completely new proposal for already in 1914 H. Bauer had drawn attention to this possibility, but the idea was only taken up by Dahood.[2] Other scholars, some of them students of Dahood, subsequently proposed further examples.[3] As the number of alleged

---

[1] M. Dahood, 'Qoheleth and Northwest Semitic Philology', *Bib* 76 (1962) 349-365:353. For further examples proposed by Dahood, cf. Martinez, *Index* I, 120; II, 135. For Dahood's examples in the Psalms, see Dahood, *Psalms* III, 375-376. The principal ones are listed by Ziony Zevit, 'The Linguistic and Contextual Arguments in Support of a Hebrew 3 m.s. Suffix *-y*', *UF* 9 (1977) 315-328. On pp. 316-318 he discusses the distribution of the 3 m.s. suffix in Phoenician-Punic.

[2] Cf. H. Bauer, 'Semitische Sprachprobleme. 4. Zum Verständnis des Status constructus und Verwandtes', *ZDMG* 68 (1914) 596- 599: 598-599. Consult W.A. van der Weiden, *Le livre des Proverbes: Notes philologiques* (BibOr 23; Rome: Pontifical Biblical Institute 1970) 84.

[3] Cf. A.C.M. Blommerde, *Northwest Semitic Grammar and Job* (BibOr 22; Pontifical Biblical Institute: Rome 1969) 8, III.1; van der Weiden, *Proverbes*, 83-85; G. del Olmo Lete, 'Notas críticas al texto hebreo de Jr. 14-17', *Claretianum* 11 (1971) 283-358: 319; L. Sabottka, *Zephanja*. Versuch einer Neuübersetzung mit philogischem Kommentar (BibOr 25; Biblical Institute Press: Rom 1972) 95-96; J. L. Crenshaw, 'Wᵉdōrēk ʿal-bāmŏtê ʾāreṣ', *CBQ* 34 (1972) 39-53:49-50; W.G.E. Watson, 'Archaic Elements in the Language of Chronicles', *Bib* 53 (1972) 191-207:202; W. Kuhnigk, *Nordwestsemitische Studien zum Hoseabuch* (BibOr 27; Biblical Institute Press: Rome 1974) 128; A. Globe, 'The Muster of the Tribes in

instances of this phenomenon increased, a systematic investigation of it became desirable and L. Boadt then wrote a study of the examples put forward for the book of Job, concluding that twenty examples supported more or less strongly the likelihood of this suffix.[4] Z. Zevit, examined those suggested for the Psalms but his view was that the argument for the suffix was 'demonstrably fragile'.[5] A brief consideration of the method employed in these two studies may help to explain their different conclusions.

Boadt's very positive approach to Ugaritic and Phoenician as aids to exegesis may be seen in his opening sentence when he observes that 'The value of Northwest Semitic studies for biblical interpretation continues to grow'.[6] One argument for the existence of the suffix is that it prevents emendation of the text, another that it helps 'to avoid contortion of the meaning'.[7] An example is Job 23,2

גַּם־הַיּוֹם מְרִי שִׂחִי יָדִי כָּבְדָה עַל־אַנְחָתִי,
Today also my complaint is bitter;
his hand is heavy in spite of my groaning. (RSV)

Judges 5 11e-18', *ZAW* 87 (1975) 169-184:170-171; T. Penar, *Northwest Semitic Philology and the Hebrew Fragments of Ben Sira* (BibOr 28; Biblical Institute Press: Rome 1975) 37; W.H. Irwin, *Isaiah 28-33 Translation with Philological Notes* (BibOr 30; Biblical Institute Press: Rome 1977) 160-161; J. Gray, 'A Cantata of the Autumn Festival: Psalm LXVIII', *JSS* 22 (1977) 2-26:17-18; A.R. Ceresko, *Job 29-31 in the Light of Northwest Semitic* (BibOr 36; Biblical Institute Press: Rome 1980) 78; R. Althann, *A Philological Analysis of Jeremiah 4-6 in the Light of Northwest Semitic* (BibOr 38; Biblical Institute Press: Rome 1983) 69; W.L. Michel, *Job in the Light of Northwest Semitic*. Vol. 1 *Prologue and First Cycle of Speeches Job 1:1 - 14:22* (BibOr 42; Biblical Institute Press: Rome 1987) 302; E. Zurro, *Procedimientos iterativos en la poesía ugarítica y hebrea* (BibOr 43; Biblical Institute Press: Rome 1987) 142.

[4] L. Boadt, 'A Re-Examination of the Third-Yodh Suffix in Job', *UF* 7 (1975) 59-72:71.

[5] Zevit, 'Arguments', *UF* 9 (1977) 328.

[6] Boadt, 'Suffix', *UF* 7 (1975) 59.

[7] Boadt, 'Suffix', *UF* 7 (1975) 71.

Boadt accepts that the suffix in יָדִי is third person, which is supported by both the LXX and the Syriac,[8] whereas for example Pope who accepts the need for a third person suffix attributes the spelling to confusion between ו and י in later orthography.[9] Boadt concludes that eleven passages in Job support very strongly the likelihood of the alleged morpheme existing in Biblical Hebrew. A brief look at these examples is in order.[10]

> אִם־לְכֹחַ אַמִּיץ הִנֵּה וְאִם־לְמִשְׁפָּט מִי יוֹעִידֵנִי (Job 9,19)
> If it is a context of strength, behold him!
> If it is a matter of justice, who can summon him? (RSV)
>
> If it be a trial of strength—he is the mighty One!
> If it be a trial at court—who will arraign him for me? (Habel)[11]

Boadt gives the translation of the RSV and comments that יוֹעִידֵנִי is 'unintelligible', unless the suffix be analysed as third person.[12] It is true that the direct object of the verb should be third person, but as Habel points out the first person suffix can be explained as dative. The direct object is omitted and needs to be supplied by the context.[13]

> אִם־אֶצְדָּק פִּי יַרְשִׁיעֵנִי (Job 9,20a)
> Though I am innocent, my own mouth would condemn me. (RSV)

[8] Boadt, 'Suffix', *UF* 7 (1975) 64.

[9] M.H. Pope, *Job*. Introduction, translation, and notes (AB 15; Doubleday: Garden City [3]1973) 171.

[10] Job 3,20 is treated on p. 143.

[11] N.C. Habel, *The Book of Job: A Commentary* (OTL; Westminster: Philadelphia 1985) 179.

[12] Boadt, 'Suffix', *UF* 7 (1975) 67.

[13] Habel, *Job*, 182.

This is a paradox and commentators sometimes try to remove it by emending the text to read a third person suffix on פִּי.[14] Dahood proposes to take the suffix as already third person.[15] Nevertheless, it is possible to accept the paradox. Job is convinced that anything he says will be used as evidence against him.[16] There would then be no reason to find a third person suffix here.

אֲדַבְּרָה וְלֹא אִירָאֶנּוּ   כִּי לֹא־כֵן אָנֹכִי עִמָּדִי (Job 9,35)
Then I would speak without fear of him,
for I am not so in myself. (RSV)

I would speak and not fear him
though I am not just before him (Blommerde)[17]

And I can state my case without fear of him.
But this is not so for me. (Habel)[18]

The meaning of the second stich is not immediately obvious and different changes have been proposed.[19] Blommerde parses the suffix on עִמָּדִי as third person,[20] but this is contrary to Job's stance throughout the speech.[21] Habel keeps the MT and accepts the first person suffix. He notes the *inclusio* of כִּי לֹא־כֵן with כִּי־כֵן in v. 2 and suggests that אָנֹכִי in v. 35 may perhaps be intended to balance יָדַעְתִּי

[14] See G. Fohrer, *Das Buch Hiob* (KAT 16; Gütersloher Verlagshaus: Gütersloh 1963) 199.

[15] M Dahood, 'Hebrew-Ugaritic Lexicography VII', *Bib* 50 (1969) 353. See too Blommerde, *Job*, 56; Boadt, 'Suffix', *UF* 7 (1975) 62; Michel, *Job*, 218 and n.115.

[16] Habel, *Job*, 193; Pope, *Job*, 73.

[17] Blommerde, *Job*, 57.

[18] Habel, *Job*, 180, see 183.

[19] Cf. Fohrer, *Hiob*, 200; Pope, *Job*, 76-77.

[20] Tentatively accepted by Michel, *Job*, 233-234. See the discussion in Boadt, 'Suffix', *UF* 7 (1975) 62.

[21] Habel, *Job*, 183.

in v. 2, the verb being double duty. Habel's is probably the most successful attempt to date at explaining the MT.

אַף־עַל־זֶה פָּקַחְתָּ עֵינֶךָ וְאֹתִי תָבִיא בְמִשְׁפָּט עִמָּךְ (Job 14,3)
And dost thou open thy eyes upon such a one,
and bring him into judgment with thee. (RSV)

The abrupt switch to the first person in the second stich is disturbing and the RSV feels constrained to employ the third person, as do the LXX, Vulgate and Peshitta. Some commentators emend the text accordingly.[22] Dahood parsed the suffix as third person.[23] Nevertheless, as Michel points out, 'the poet has Job quite often oscillating between his own tragic lot and that of all humans'.[24] The technique is common in Northwest Semitic literature, often as a means of drawing the audience's attention to something that should affect them personally.

כִּי תֹאמְרוּ מַה־נִּרְדָּף־לוֹ וְשֹׁרֶשׁ דָּבָר נִמְצָא־בִי (Job 19,28)
If you say, 'How we will pursue him!'
and, 'The root of the matter is found in him'. (RSV)

If ye say, 'How will we persecute him!'
and *that* the root of the matter is found
in me. (Driver - Gray)

The emendation to the third person suffix in the second stich practised by the RSV is common.[25] Dahood followed by Blommerde parses the

[22] Cf. Driver - Gray, *Job* II, 88; Fohrer, *Hiob*, 239.

[23] M. Dahood in a review of G. Garbini, *Il semitico di nord-ovest*, in *Or* n.s. 32 (1963) 499. See too Blommerde, *Job*, 69; Boadt, 'Suffix', *UF* 7 (1975) 67.

[24] Michel, *Job*, 317.

[25] See Fohrer, *Hiob*, 309; Habel, *Job*, 294.

suffix of the MT as third person.[26] Driver and Gray observe that there is in the MT a change from direct speech in the first stich to indirect in the second.[27] The MT is grammatically sound and the difficulty is rather one of style. The abrupt shift to indirect speech is very effective in making Job's point that he personally is the victim. It may be noticed that in every verse of the chapter, except vv. 24 and 29, a first person suffix is found.

הֵן לֹא בְיָדָם טוּבָם   עֲצַת רְשָׁעִים רָחֲקָה מֶנִּי (Job 21,16)
Behold is not their prosperity in their hand?
The counsel of the wicked is far from me. (RSV)

Our happiness is certainly not his doing,
(The counsel of the wicked is beyond me!) (Habel)

Is not from his hands their prosperity?
Still, the council of the wicked is far from him. (Blommerde)[28]

The two stichs lie awkwardly together on the rendering of the RSV and the second is sometimes treated as out of place.[29] Habel treats the first stich as a continuation of the words of the wicked in vv. 14-15, v. 16b is then a personal disclaimer by Job.[30] At the same time

[26] M. Dahood, 'Northwest Semitic Philology and Job', *Gruenthaner Memorial Volume: The Bible in Current Catholic Thought* (ed. J.L. McKenzie) (Saint Mary's Theology Studies 8; Herder and Herder: New York 1962) 62; Blommerde, *Job*, 89. See too Boadt, 'Suffix', *UF* 7 (1975) 68.

[27] Driver - Gray, *Job* II, 132. At the same time they prefer to read the third person as being more forcible.

[28] Blommerde, *Job*, 92 where an alternative rendering is also proposed, 'Behold, the Mighty One (*lē'?*), from his hands is their prosperity, though the council of the wicked is far from him'. See too Boadt, 'Suffix', *UF* 7 (1975) 63.

[29] See Driver - Gray, *Job* I, 185. The second stich appears again in 22,18b. The whole verse is taken as a gloss to vv. 14-15 by Fohrer, *Hiob*, 338, as out of place by Pope, *Job*, 158-159.

[30] Habel, *Job*, 327-328.

he changes the suffix of טוֹבָם (judged to be a scribal error) to first person plural.[31] Blommerde understands the whole verse as words of Job. בְּיָדָם is revocalised בְּיָדֵם, parsed as a contracted northern dual. There is no suffix either because it is a part of the body which frequently lacks a suffix, or because the suffix of the following מֶנִּי is double duty. Even if one accepts the grammar of this explanation, the thought is prosaic. It may still be safest to accept the MT and to admit that different explanations of the first stich are possible. A poetic line may well be susceptible of more than one interpretation, not necessarily even consciously intended by the author.

גַּם־הַיּוֹם מְרִי שִׂחִי יָדִי כָּבְדָה עַל־אַנְחָתִי (Job 23,2)
Today also my complaint is bitter;
his hand is heavy in spite of my groaning. (RSV)

The RSV with many authorities smooths the verse by changing the suffix of יָדִי to third person. Dahood and Blommerde judge this to be another example of the third person suffix in -*y*.[32] Nonetheless, the first person suffix on יָדִי would fit the context if Job were trying to suppress his groaning, 'My hand is heavy upon my groaning'.[33] It may be objected that this is a contrived answer, but in the book of Job there are frequent grammatical and stylistic surprises.

עַל־מִשְׁפָּטִי אֲכַזֵּב אָנוּשׁ חִצִּי בְלִי־פָשַׁע (Job 34,6)
In spite of my right I am counted a liar;
my wound is incurable, though I am without transgression. (RSV)

V.6b Wounded with his darts, yet sinless. (Blommerde)[34]

---

[31] Habel, *Job*, 322.

[32] Dahood, *Gruenthaner Memorial Volume*, 62; Blommerde, *Job*, 99. See Boadt, 'Suffix', *UF* 7 (1975) 64.

[33] See Driver - Gray, *Job* II, 160.

[34] Blommerde, *Job*, 120-121, reading חִצַּי for MT חִצִּי.

To render חִצִּי 'my arrow' would not be acceptable and different emendations of the consonantal text have been proposed.[35] Blommerde proposes to see here a third person suffix in *-y* and is followed by Boadt and Habel.[36] At the same time חִצִּי can be understood as 'my arrow-wound', a metonymy that is unexceptionable and refers back to 6,4.[37]

לֹא־אַכְזָר כִּי יְעוּרֶנּוּ וּמִי הוּא לְפָנַי יִתְיַצָּב (Job 41,2)
No one is so fierce that he dares to stir him up.
Who then is he that can stand before me? (RSV [41,10])

No one is as fierce as to arouse him,
and who then can stand before him? (Blommerde)[38]

The sudden introduction of God in the second stich causes commentators difficulty and leads to emendations.[39] Blommerde tries to eliminate the difficulty by parsing the suffix of לְפָנַי as third person. Habel on the other hand maintains strongly that the suffix is first person:

> To change the first person forms of this verse to third person is unwarranted; to do so ignores the flexible style of the poet, previous first person indicators in this speech (40:8,14,15), and a direct allusion to earlier demands of Job.[40]

[35] See Fohrer, *Hiob*, 464; Pope, *Job*, 256.
[36] Cf. Boadt, 'Suffix', *UF* 7 (1975) 65; Habel, *Job*, 475.
[37] See Driver - Gray, *Job* I, 295.
[38] Blommerde, *Job*, 137. See Dahood, *Psalms* I, 11, 115, 168; Boadt, 'Suffix', *UF* 7 (1975) 65.
[39] See Fohrer, *Hiob*, 527; Pope, *Job*, 337 [at v. 11].
[40] Habel, *Job*, 555.

V.3 continues with God as the speaker, and the first person suffix is supported by the ancient Versions.[41] The sudden switch of persons may be unacceptable to the modern reader, but here again the problem is one of style rather than grammar.

This examination of some of the stronger examples of the alleged third person singular suffix in -*y* in the book of Job shows that other explanations of the phenomenon are possible. Hence, these passages cannot be employed to demonstrate that it is found in Biblical Hebrew.

2. The 3 m.s. Suffix in Northwest Semitic and the Variation between qere-ketib

Zevit too has examined instances of the alleged suffix but in the Psalms. He finds five examples in Psalms where the explanation of this suffix as 3 m.s. is possible, noting that in three of them the LXX translated a 3 m.s. suffix. Zevit, however, argues that

> the *yodhs* in each of the five possible examples from Psalms may be explained as having arisen due to the erroneous resolution of a *waw* grapheme.[42]

With regard to the evidence of the LXX, he argues that the Hebrew Vorlage may have been different or at least palaeographically ambiguous.[43] Zevit's approach is highly cautious. He evaluates the proposed examples of the suffix in Psalms 'as being either possible, possible but not necessary, possible but highly improbable, or impossible'.[44] It can be seen that there is no category 'probable',

---

[41] See the discussion by Driver in Driver - Gray, *Job* I, 363-364 [at v. 11a].

[42] Zevit, 'Arguments', *UF* 9 (1977) 328.

[43] Zevit, 'Arguments', *UF* 9 (1977) 327.

[44] Zevit, 'Arguments', *UF* 9 (1977) 318.

which contrasts with Boadt who employs 'probable' and 'highly probable'.[45]

Zevit's approach is influenced by a number of factors. First, he finds the evidence for the existence of this suffix in Ugaritic which features *-h* as the normal 3 m.s. suffix, 'equivocal at best'.[46]

The morpheme is on the other hand well attested in Phoenician-Punic. Cross and Freedman have argued that the evidence of the non-Byblian Phoenician inscriptions indicates two 3 m.s. suffixes. After analysing their distribution they conclude that

> the suffix appears as *yodh* in the orthography with nouns or verbs ending with long vowels, and with singular nouns in the *genitive case*; with nouns in the *accusative case*, the suffix appears as zero in the orthography.[47]

Krahmalkov studied the distribution of the three 3 m.s. suffixes attested in Punic, *-y*, *-m* and *-ʾ*.[48] He found that *-m* was employed with the genitive and *-ʾ* with nouns which are the direct objects of verbs and are not preceded by the accusative particle. Zevit after referring to Krahmalkov's conclusions emphasises that

> the different orthographic representations, or lack of representation, of the 3 m.s. suffix are to be segregated both synchronically and diachronically and that within each

[45] Boadt, 'Suffix', *UF* 7 (1975) 71.

[46] Zevit, 'Arguments', *UF* 9 (1977) 316. The reading *ṯbty* in KTU 1.5(67).II:16 turns out to be erroneous. The alleged suffix is not present (the revised *KTU* [p. 23a] restores a missing sign: *ṯbt*<h>). This text therefore cannot be adduced in support of the alleged suffix in Ugaritic.

[47] The vowel being probably *ô*. See F.M. Cross - D.N. Freedman, 'The Pronominal Suffixes of the Third Person Singular in Phoenician', *JNES* 10 (1951) 228-230:229.

[48] C.R. Krahmalkov, 'Studies in Phoenician and Punic Grammar', *JSS* 15 (1970) 181-188:185-188.

> dialect their employment was not random but highly structured.[49]

Krahmalkov noted, however, that *-m* and *-y* appear as variant genitive suffixes in the inscriptions from El-Hofra which feature *lmlky*, (56.4, 57.4f, 58.4, 61.4, 62) and *lmlkm* (59.4/5, 60.5, 64.3) 'of his reign'.[50] It can be seen that the two genitive suffixes may be employed with the same noun in the same text.[51] El-Hofra 121 provides another example of the two suffixes employed in the same text:

> *ʾdnbʿl bn ʿbdšḥ ndr lʾdny bʿl ḥmn šlm ʾt ndrm šm qlʾ*
> ʿIdnibal, son of Abdshaḥ, made a vow to his lord, Baal-Ḥammon; he fulfilled his vow, (for) he heard his voice.[52]

The Phoenician Aḥiram inscription from Byblos (KAI 1) contains the suffix ה-. Soon, however, from the time of Yeḥimilk, the Byblos inscriptions employ ו-.[53]

Standard grammars of Biblical Hebrew recognise four different representations of the 3 m.s. suffix.[54] There is ו after plural nouns.[55]

---

[49] 'Arguments', *UF* 9 (1977) 318.

[50] Krahmalkov, 'Studies', *JSS* 15 (1970) 186.

[51] Krahmalkov judges the suffixal form *-y* 'to be archaizing and not indicative of normative Punic usage', cf. id., 'Studies', *JSS* 15 (1970) 186.

[52] Krahmalkov, 'Studies', *JSS* 15 (1970) 187. Cf. A. Berthier - R. Charlier, *Le sanctuaire punique d'El-Hofra à Constantine* (Paris: Arts et Métiers Graphiques 1955) 96.

[53] J. Friedrich - W. Röllig, *Phönizisch-Punische Grammatik* (AnOr 46; Pontificium Institutum Biblicum: Roma [2]1970) #112; S. Segert, *A Grammar of Phoenician and Punic* (Beck: München 1976) 97 #51.221.

[54] Cf. *GKC*, #91b-e; Joüon - Muraoka, *Grammar*, #94h.

[55] See the discussion in Joüon - Muraoka, *Grammar*, #94d n.2.

After singular nouns, beside the spelling ־וֹ, there is the older ־ה, where the ה represents the *h* of the primitive form *ahū*. Joüon and Muraoka observe that the spelling כֻּלֹּה is as common as כֻּלּוֹ, but that in other cases the qere sometimes prescribes וֹ, e.g. for אָהֳלֹה in Gen 9,21; 12,8; 13,3; 35,21. In addition there is the suffix ־הוּ of III-He nouns, which also features in other nouns: רֵעֵהוּ (except Jer 6,21 רֵעוֹ) from רֵעַ, 'companion'. Joüon and Muraoka further note לְמִינֵהוּ in Gen 1,12.21.25, but לְמִינוֹ in v. 11.[56]

It can be seen that Hebrew and Phoenician overlap to some extent in their graphic representation of the 3 m.s. suffix. Hebrew like the dialect of Byblos employs ־ה and ־ו. Its use of *-ô* probably finds a parallel in the non-Byblian dialects, even if this suffix is not represented graphically. It must nevertheless be asked how far the Phoenician evidence is relevant for Biblical Hebrew. If Phoenician and Hebrew are distinct languages, its relevance is slight. If on the other hand these languages are in reality merely dialects of a larger grouping, as Dahood believed, then the evidence of Phoenician becomes more important. There are different views on the matter, but until it is demonstrated that Phoenician is only dialectally distinct from Hebrew, the Phoenician evidence cannot be considered relevant to the question of whether or not a 3 s. suffix in *-y* exists in Biblical Hebrew. The case for the alleged morpheme then stands or falls by the evidence of Hebrew texts.

Zevit refers to the 'more than 50 cases' in which qere and ketib differ in their choice of *waw* and *yod*. According to one study there are 48 words which the ketib terminates in *waw*, the qere in *yod*, and 24 words in which the reverse is true.[57] These quite numerous variations of final *waw*, final *yod* in the ketib-qere shed little light on the question of whether or not a third person suffix singular in *yod*

---

[56] Joüon - Muraoka, *Grammar*, #94h.

[57] Cf. S. Bamberger, 'Die Bedeutung der Qeri Kethib, ein Beitrag zur Geschichte der Exegese', *Jahrbuch der Jüdisch-Literarischen Gesellschaft* 15 (1923) 226-227 and notes 1 and 2 on p. 227.

exists. If corruption of the text took place, it would have been before the ketib-qere notations were developed.[58] Two instances of ketib: final *waw*, qere: final *yod* may nevertheless be briefly considered.

> לֹא־תִשְׁתַּחֲוֶה לָהֶם וְלֹא תָעָבְדֵם כִּי אָנֹכִי יְהוָה אֱלֹהֶיךָ
> אֵל קַנָּא פֹּקֵד עֲוֹן אָבוֹת עַל־בָּנִים
> וְעַל־שִׁלֵּשִׁים וְעַל־רִבֵּעִים לְשֹׂנְאָי׃
> וְעֹשֶׂה חֶסֶד לַאֲלָפִים לְאֹהֲבַי
> וּלְשֹׁמְרֵי מצותו (Deut 5,9-10)
>
> you shall not bow down to them or serve them; for I the LORD your God am a jealous God, visiting the iniquity of the fathers upon the children to the third and fourth generation of those who hate me, (10) but showing steadfast love to thousands of those who love me and keep my commandments. (RSV)

In v. 10 for the ketib מצותו, the qere proposes מצותי which is the reading in the parallel passage in Exod 20,6. Consistency does appear to require a first person suffix in view of the preceding לְאֹהֲבַי. On the other hand the following verse speaks of the Lord in the third person. The ketib can in point of fact be retained when it is remembered that court style allows the superior to be addressed or to refer to himself in the third person. Furthermore, the abrupt switching of persons is a feature of Hebrew rhetorical style. Both qere and ketib are 'correct', and the difference is to be attributed to stylistic considerations. There is no need to postulate a third person suffix in *-y*.

The second example is from Isaiah

> וְעַמֵּךְ כֻּלָּם צַדִּיקִים לְעוֹלָם יִירְשׁוּ אָרֶץ

---

[58] Cf. Zevit, 'Arguments', *UF* 9 (1977) 327-328.

נֵצֶר מטעו [מטעי] מַעֲשֵׂה יָדַי לְהִתְפָּאֵר (Isa 60,21)
Your people shall all be righteous;
they shall possess the land for ever,
the shoot of my planting, the work of my hands,
that I might be glorified. (RSV)

1QIsa[a] and *1QIsa*[b] read ידיו for ידי and the LXX with χειρῶν αὐτοῦ points to the same Vorlage.[59] In view of the parallel מטעו (ketib), the Qumran and LXX reading of a third person suffix appears more logical. The omission of the *waw* in the MT requires explanation. The Massoretes' pointing יָדַ֣י harmonises with מטעי of the qere and of *1QIsa*[a]; *1QIsa*[b] reads מטעיו. Nevertheless, here too the ketib can be followed when the phenomena of court style and Hebrew rhetorical style are recalled. In the previous verse the Lord speaks of himself in the third person and now both first and third person are employed: 'the branch of his planting (מטעו ketib), the work of my hands (ידי)'. Once again, there is no need to postulate a third person suffix in *-y*.

Zevit further employs the argument that confusion in the orthography can explain the cases where final *yod* appears to represent the 3 m.s. suffix.[60] The letters *waw* and *yod* were written in very similar fashion during the late Hasmonaean and early Herodian periods and consequently there is indeed a possibility that these letters were confused in the script and that a final ו- suffix was read as י-.[61] This argument would not, however, apply to cases where the 3 s. suffix is feminine.[62]

---

[59] Cf. M. Burrows, *The Dead Sea scrolls of St. Mark's Monastery* (ASOR: New Haven 1950) pl. xlix; E.L. Sukenik, *The Dead Sea Scrolls of the Hebrew University* (Magnes Press: Hebrew University Jerusalem 1955) pl. xiii.

[60] Zevit, 'Arguments', *UF* 9 (1977) 327.

[61] Cf. F.M. Cross, 'The Development of the Jewish Scripts', *The Bible and the Ancient Near East*. Essays in Honor of William Foxwell Albright (ed. G.E. Wright) (Doubleday: Garden City 1961) 133-202:169-170, 176.

[62] Cf. M. Dahood, 'Hebrew-Ugaritic Lexicography II', *Bib* 45 (1964) 393-412:397 n.2; id., 'A Note on Third Person Suffix *-y* in Hebrew', *UF* 4 (1972) 163-164:163.

3. A 3 f.s. suffix in -*y*?

It has been suggested that one example of the 3 f.s. suffix in -*y* may occur in Job 3,10

> כִּי לֹא סָגַר דַּלְתֵי בִטְנִי וַיַּסְתֵּר עָמָל מֵעֵינָי
> Because it did not shut the doors of her womb
> nor avert trouble from my eyes. (Dahood)[63]

The LXX offers

> *ὅτι οὐ συνέκλεισεν πύλας γαστρὸς μητρός μου·*
> *ἀπήλλαξεν γὰρ ἂν πόνον ἀπὸ ὀφθαλμῶν μου.*
> Because it did not shut the doors of my mother's womb for it would have removed sorrow from my eyes.

A number of translators follow the LXX and understand בִטְנִי as 'my womb' in the sense of the womb which bore me; so the NRSV, 'my mother's womb'.[64] The phrase פְּרִי בִטְנִי, 'the fruit of my body' referring to the father appears in Mic 6,7 parallel to בְּכוֹרִי, 'my first-born', but in Job 3,10 the expression דַּלְתֵי בִטְנִי refers to the womb. The formulation is quite unusual and the poet's choice of the -*y* suffix will have been dictated by special considerations, whether it is first person or third.

---

[63] Cf. M. Dahood, 'Northwest Semitic Texts and Textual Criticism of the Hebrew Bible', *Questions disputées d'Ancien Testament*. Méthode et théologie (ed. C. Brekelmans) (BETL 33; Leuven University Press: Leuven 1974) 11-37: 21, 25. A further step is to take the suffix of מֵעֵינָי as third person, see Michel, *Job*, 60.

[64] Cf. Driver - Gray, *Job* I, 35; *WOC*, 148 n.26. For an overview of the various proposals, cf. Michel, *Job*, 60 n.110, 111.

In the first place it should be observed that the suffix is not strictly necessary. בטן clearly refers to Job's mother. If a suffix is added it must be for a particular reason. In fact the *î* sound appears twice in the first stich, while the related *ê* occurs once. In the second stich *î* is not found, but *ê* is repeated three times and the final suffix in מֵעֵינָי yields a similar sound. The recurrence of these sounds is part of the poet's art, and in this the suffix of בִטְנִי plays a part. There may also be another reason why the poet avoids employing a word for mother in this verse. In the course of the chapter there are allusions to her in several verses (vv. 3, 10, 11, 12, 16) but no direct reference. The emphasis is rather on the misery of the hero. Hence, it would in fact be inappropriate to indicate her directly in v. 10, as does the LXX. The phrase 'my womb' is no doubt elliptical for the prosaic, 'the womb of my mother', but ellipsis is a marked characteristic of Hebrew poetry. The form of בִטְנִי then may be explained without postulating a third person suffix in *-y*.

A similar question arises in 19,17

רוּחִי זָרָה לְאִשְׁתִּי וְחַנֹּתִי לִבְנֵי בִטְנִי
Foreign to my wife is my spirit,
and my supplication to the sons of her womb. (Dahood)[65]

The LXX renders

καὶ ἱκέτευον τὴν γυναῖκά μου,
προσεκαλούμην δὲ κολακεύων υἱοὺς παλλακίδων μου
And I besought my wife,
and earnestly entreated the sons of my concubines.

[65] Cf. Dahood, 'Northwest Semitic Texts', *BETL* 33, 25.

It can be seen that for לִבְנֵי בִטְנִי the LXX has *υἱοὺς παλλακίδων μου*. Since בֶּטֶן does sometimes denote a man's body there is in fact no real difficulty in this verse. It is only the similarity to 3,10 that creates one. If there is no need to postulate a third person suffix in *-y* for 3,10, this is *a fortiori* true of 19,17.

Another passage which has been thought to witness to the 3 f.s. suffix in *-y* is Jer 51,1

> הִנְנִי מֵעִיר עַל־בָּבֶל וְאֶל־יֹשְׁבֵי לֵב קָמָי
> Behold, I am arousing against Babylon and against her inhabitants the courage of her assailants... (Dahood)[66]

It is especially the suffix of קָמָי that requires explanation. 'Those rising up *against me*' makes no sense in the context of the Lord raising up enemies against Babylon. Dahood parses the suffix as third person and also feminine, בָּבֶל being of this gender (see v. 2). Commentators generally take לֵב קָמָי as an athbash or cypher for כַּשְׂדִּים, observing that the LXX renders Χαλδαίους.[67] If the purpose of the athbash was to conceal the reference from the uninitiated, the mention of Babylon earlier in the same verse would make a cypher unnecessary.[68] S.B. Noegel argues, however, that since for the ancients words contained in concentrated form their referents, the athbash represents a reversal of their essence. In other words the athbash in Jer 51,1 indicates the destruction of Babylon. The context is one of a power struggle and '*atbash* typically occurs in contexts in

---

66 M. Dahood, 'The Integrity of Jeremiah 51,1', *Bib* 53 (1972) 542.

67 See, for instance, J. Bright, *Jeremiah*. Introduction, Translation, and Notes (AB 21; Doubleday: Garden City 1965) 355. 'Athbash' is a type of 'cryptographic scheme in which the letters of the alphabet in reverse were substituted': א for ת, ב for ש and so on. Cf. B.J. Roberts, 'Athbash', *IDB* I, 306-307.

68 Cf. R.P. Carroll, *Jeremiah*. A Commentary (OTL; SCM: London 1986) 837-838.

which power struggles take place'.[69] R.C. Steiner notes that in late antiquity the athbash was a well known phenomenon in school exercises. In Jeremiah 51 it has 'the effect of flouting the taboo against anti-Babylonian agitation'.[70] While these arguments do not exclude Dahood's proposal, they do weaken its cogency. There are consequently no clear examples of a final *yod* representing the 3 f.s. ending. Orthographic confusion between י and ו cannot be ruled out to explain some other alleged examples of the phenomenon. The existence in Biblical Hebrew of a 3 s. suffix in -*y* has therefore not been demonstrated.[71] At the same time the quest for the alleged morpheme was not in vain if it stimulated closer attention to the Hebrew text and to the literary style of its authors.

---

[69] S.B. Noegel, 'Atbash (אתב"ש) in Jeremiah and Its Literary Significance—Part 1', *Jewish Bible Quarterly* 24 (1996) 82-89:84.

[70] R.C. Steiner, 'The two sons of Neriah and the two editions of Jeremiah in the light of two *atbash* code-words for Babylon', *VT* 46 (1996) 74-84, esp. 81-84.

[71] For further proposed examples of the 3 s. suffix in -*y*, cf. Dahood, 'A Note', *UF* 4 (1972) 163: 2 Sam 22,34 בָּמוֹתַי 'his heights'; Hos 11,1 לִבְנִי 'to his sons'; Zeph 2,14 גוי 'in her midst' (see Sabottka, *Zephanja*, 95-96); Zech 12,10 אֵלַי 'upon him'; Ps 7,5 צוֹרְרִי 'his enemy'; Job 10,1 עָלַי 'before Him'; 31,18 מִנְּעוּרַי 'since his youth'; 32,14 אֵלַי 'against him'; 41,2 לְפָנַי 'before his face; Lam 1,3 מֵעֹנִי 'because of her iniquity'; 1,9 עָנְיִי 'her affliction'.

5

A Review of the Evidence for *p*, 'and' in Biblical Hebrew

Several Semitic languages witness to a conjunction *p*, 'and' which is employed with different nuances.[1] Some scholars have argued that it may also be found in Classical Hebrew.[2] On the other hand K. Aartun subjected seven of the proposed examples to analysis and concluded that the particle was not present.[3] Nevertheless, Waltke and O'Connor remark that the issue is not settled.[4] It may therefore be worthwhile to consider again the arguments for the presence or otherwise of this particle in the Hebrew scriptures. Only those examples will be considered that have actually been discussed.

---

[1] The particle occurs in Ugaritic, Old Aramaic, Samalian, Nabataean, Palmyrene, Old South Arabian languages and Classical Arabic, cf. W.G.E. Watson, 'The Particle *p* in Ugaritic,' *SEL* 7 (1990) 75-86: 83; id., 'Ugaritic *p* Again', *UF* 24 (1994) 493-495.

[2] M. Dahood was a leading proponent of Hebrew *p*, 'and', consult Dahood, *Psalms* III, 410; Martinez, *Index* II, 130. See too the bibliography in Blommerde, *Job*, 32-33.

[3] K. Aartun, 'Textüberlieferung und vermeintliche Belege der Konjunktion *pV* im Alten Testament,' *UF* 10 (1978) 1-13.

[4] *WOC*, 655. See too Watson, *SEL* 7 (1990) 83 n.49.

1. Psalms and Job

כִּי־לִי כָל־חַיְתוֹ־יָעַר
בְּהֵמוֹת בְּהַרְרֵי־אָלֶף (Ps 50,10)
For every beast of the forest is mine,
the cattle on a thousand hills. (RSV)

For every beast of the forest is mine,
the cattle upon the mighty mountains;
(v. 11) *For* I know all the fowl of the mountains... (Dahood)[5]

The RSV understands the number as qualifying בְּהַרְרֵי. In view of the apparent parallelism between כָל and אֶלֶף, other translations take אֶלֶף with בְּהֵמוֹת, 'cattle in thousands' (NEB, see too NAB). Another possibility is to assign the meaning 'cattle' to אֶלֶף as does the LXX, *κτήνη ἐν τοῖς ὄρεσιν καὶ βόες*, 'the cattle on the mountains, and oxen'. Aartun points out that there is formal parallelism between כָל־חַיְתוֹ־יָעַר and בְּהֵמוֹת בְּהַרְרֵי־אָלֶף, and that חַיְתוֹ־יָעַר is balanced by בְּהֵמוֹת בְּהַרְרֵי.[6] Since כָל is evidently an expression of quantity, the corresponding word in the next stich should also imply this. Hence אֶלֶף signifies 'thousand' rather than 'cattle'. The construction בְּהַרְרֵי־אָלֶף follows a well-attested pattern, the governed noun expressing an epexegetical genitive. Hence he would render 'on the thousand mountains'. Nonetheless, there is a difficulty. While there are in Biblical Hebrew several instances of a number in this position, all the examples put forward show the number functioning as an ordinal, which would clearly be inappropriate here. Commentators are in general reluctant to accept the MT. Craigie suggests הַרְרֵי־אֵל, 'marvelous mountains,' while Kraus reads בְּהַרְרֵי־אֵל, 'auf den

[5] M. Dahood, 'Some Northwest-Semitic Words in Job,' *Bib* 38 (1957) 312.
[6] Aartun, 'Textüberlieferung', *UF* 10 (1978) 5.

"Gottesbergen",' as in Ps 36,7.[7] Dahood's suggestion is to transfer the פ of אֶלֶף to the following word so as to read הַרְרֵי־אֵל פִּיָדַעְתִּי. This would harmonise with the views of Craigie and Kraus, while allowing the consonantal text to remain intact. Here then the assumption of a morpheme פ, 'and' is attractive.

הֵן יַחְתֹּף מִי יְשִׁיבֶנּוּ
מִי־יֹאמַר אֵלָיו מַה־תַּעֲשֶׂה (Job 9,12)
Behold, he snatches away; who can hinder him?
Who will say to him, 'What doest thou'? (RSV)

If He should snatch away, who could resist Him? (Dahood)[8]

Dahood later changed his mind on this verse,[9] but since his first proposal has received some support, it will be considered here.[10] Dahood points out that among the ancient versions 'there is no agreement as to the precise significance of [יַחְתֹּף], which as a verbal form is a hapax legomenon'. There is similar disagreement among modern translators who sometimes emend it to יַחְטֹף.[11] Dahood's proposal to read הֵן יַחְתֹּף מִי replaces an otherwise unattested verb with a securely attested one: חתה, 'remove, snatch away'. It preserves the consonantal text but does suppose the existence of a conjunction פ. Aartun argues that the root חתף is attested as a noun in Prov 23,28

---

[7] Cf. Craigie, *Psalms 1-50*, 363; Kraus, *Psalmen* I, 525, 526.

[8] Dahood, 'Northwest-Semitic Words', *Bib* 38 (1957) 310.

[9] Cf. M. Dahood, 'Ugaritic and Phoenician or Qumran and the Versions,' *Orient and Occident*. Essays Presented to Cyrus H. Gordon on the Occasion of His Sixty-fifth Birthday (ed. H.A. Hoffner) (AOAT 22; Butzon & Bercker: Kevelaer 1973) 55.

[10] See the discussion in Pope, *Job*, 72-73.

[11] The nominal form but not the verbal form is discussed by G. Rinaldi, 'Studi italiani sul testo ebraico anticotestamentario,' *BeO* 22 (1980) 62.

with the sense, 'robber' and that the verb חטף has a similar meaning in Ps 10,9, points also mentioned by Dahood.[12] Aartun shows that these roots are also found in other Semitic languages and concludes that the form יַחְתֹּף does not present any linguistic difficulty.[13] Dahood offered his suggestion 'as a mere possibility,' but it would become more than that if the existence of a conjunction פ could be demonstrated from other texts.

אִם־אֶצְדָּק פִּי יַרְשִׁיעֵנִי תָּם־אָנִי וַיַּעְקְשֵׁנִי (Job 9,20)
Though I am innocent, my own mouth would condemn me;
though I am blameless, he would prove me perverse. (RSV)

If I am innocent, He will declare me guilty;
If I am blameless, He will find me perverse. (Dahood)[14]

The translation of the RSV does not completely satisfy. Why should my own mouth condemn me if I am innocent? Dahood analyses the second stich as a conditional clause whose apodosis is introduced by *waw*.[15] He argues that 'The requirements of syntax call for a

---

[12] See also Sir 15,14; 32,21; 50,4 and the discussion by L. Grabbe, *Comparative Philology and the Text of Job* (SBLDS 34; Scholars: Missoula 1977) 60-62.

[13] Aartun, 'Textüberlieferung', *UF* 10 (1978) 7-8. On p. 8 he gives the following examples: Old Arabian *ḫaṭafa/ḫaṭifa* 'wegschnappen, rauben'/ *ḫatfun* 'Tod' (<Wegreißen o.ä.); Jewish Aramaic *ḥăṭaf* 'fortreißen, rauben'/*ḥăṭaf* 'wegreißen'. He also compares Syriac *ḥĕṭaf* 'rapuit'/*ḥattef* 'fregit, confregit'.

[14] Dahood, 'Northwest-Semitic Words', *Bib* 38 (1957) 311-312; Aartun, 'Textüberlieferung', *UF* 10 (1978) 8-9.

[15] Dahood, 'Northwest-Semitic Words', *Bib* 38 (1957) 311-312; Aartun, 'Textüberlieferung', *UF* 10 (1978) 8-9.

conjunction to introduce the apodosis in the first colon, just as the apodosis is introduced by a *wāw* in the second'. The missing conjunction he finds concealed in the Massoretic פִּי. Hence, he would read פִּיַרְשִׁיעֵנִי for the Massoretes' פִּי יַרְשִׁיעֵנִי. This yields excellent parallelism and makes good sense. It does however require the deletion of one *yod* and lacks support in the textual tradition of the verse. Aartun offers a different analysis: פִּי יַרְשִׁיעֵנִי is a composite nominal clause and requires no conjunction; וַיַּעְקְשֵׁנִי is a verbal clause whose *waw* is an integral part of the imperfect consecutive and not a *waw* of apodosis.[16] Clines agrees with Aartun and adds that the parallelism is preserved if the subject of וַיַּעְקְשֵׁנִי is 'my mouth'.[17] This is true but the question of why 'my own mouth would condemn me' remains. For Dahood the appeal to Job 15,6 יַרְשִׁיעֲךָ פִיךָ וְלֹא־אָנִי 'Your own mouth condemns you, and not I' fails because the context is quite different. It would seem that a fully satisfactory explanation of the verse has yet to be given, and Dahood's proposal remains a possibility, provided that support for the existence of the alleged conjunction פ may be gleaned from other texts.[18]

יִפְרְצֵנִי פֶרֶץ עַל־פְּנֵי־פָרֶץ יָרֻץ עָלַי כְּגִבּוֹר (Job 16,14)
He breaks me with breach upon breach;
he runs upon me like a warrior. (RSV)

He breaches me with a breach in front of me,
And charging he charges me like a warrior. (Dahood)[19]

---

[16] Consult also Driver - Gray, *Job* II, 58- 59.

[17] D. Clines, *Job 1-20* (WBC 17; Dallas: Word Books, 1989) 218.

[18] Dahood's proposal is judged plausible by D.A. Robertson, *Linguistic Evidence in Dating Early Hebrew Poetry* (SBLDS 3; Society of Biblical Literature: Missoula 1972) 130: 'While some residue of doubt remains, it must be admitted that this last suggestion is the most facile way of handling the text'.

[19] Dahood, *Psalms I*, 308; id., 'Hebrew-Ugaritic Lexicography VIII', *Bib* 51 (1970) 394.

G.B. Gray remarks that פְּנֵי 'is strange', but there is no real grammatical difficulty in the verse.[20] Dahood's first proposal is to read עַל־פָּנַי פָּרֹץ (MT עַל־פְּנֵי־פָרֶץ), linking the two stichs with the conjunction פ. He subsequently also revocalizes the first פֶּרֶץ to פָּרֹץ. Only now does he explain the alterations to the MT

> From this vocalisation emerges the chiasmus of verb plus infinitive absolute, [יִפְרְצֵנִי פָּרֹץ], and infinitive absolute plus verb [רֹץ יָרֻץ]. By employing the conjunction *pa, the poet created a wordplay on [פָּרֹץ], "breaching", and [פָּרֹץ], "and charging"...the 3+3 beat and the 9:9 syllable count that result from the new reading are preferable to the 4+3 beat and the 11:7 syllable count of MT.[21]

Aartun argues that the structure of the two stichs is normal in Hebrew.[22] Dahood's reasons are in fact stylistic rather than grammatical so that while interesting they will not in the view of most outweigh the witness of the tradition represented by the MT.

2. Canticle 3,10

תּוֹכוֹ רָצוּף אַהֲבָה מִבְּנוֹת יְרוּשָׁלָםִ (Cant 3,10b)

It was lovingly wrought within by the daughters of Jerusalem. (RSV)[23]

---

[20] Cf. Driver - Gray, *Job* II, 106.

[21] For the word order of finite verb - infinitive absolute he refers to Job 13,17; 21,2; Gen 8,7.

[22] Aartun, 'Textüberlieferung', *UF* 10 (1978) 9. Aartun does not refer to Dahood's second proposal.

[23] M. Dahood, *Proverbs and Northwest Semitic Philology* (Scripta Pontificii Instituti Biblici 113; Pontificium Institutum Biblicum: Roma 1963) 54 n.7 (pp. 53-54).

ἐντὸς αὐτοῦ λιθόστρωτον ἀγάπην ἀπὸ θυγατέρων Ιερουσαλη (LXX)
within it a pavement, (a gift/sign of) love by the daughters of Jerusalem.

One difficulty lies in the hapaxlegomenon רָצוּף. The RSV associates it with the noun רִצְפָּה, 'pavement', following the LXX's *λιθόστρωτον*. The LXX would seem to have had the same Vorlage as the MT. Gerleman argues that the sense of *ἀγάπη* supposed by the LXX ('Liebeserweisung', 'Liebesgabe') is not otherwise attested in pre-Christian times, and he prefers to alter אַהֲבָה to אֲבָנִים, 'its interior is adorned with stones'.[24]

Dahood reads תּוֹכוֹ רָצוֹ פְּאַהֲבָה, 'Within it there is pleasure and love,' parsing רָצוֹ as infinitive absolute with the Northern or Phoenician spelling, while the particle פ is attached to the following word.[25] He does not explain why he makes the change, but it can be surmised that he tried to eliminate a hapaxlegomenon and elicit a straightforward meaning from a difficult text. The verb רצה I, 'be pleased with' is common, and the infinitive absolute with *û* probably occurs even outside the hollow verbs.[26]

Aartun notes that the textual tradition does not give evidence of a different text.[27] He analyses the syntagma as a nominal clause, consisting of subject ([תּוֹכוֹ]) and predicate ([רָצוּף]) plus a further determination ([אַהֲבָה]). This last element relates to either the predicate alone or to the whole sentence. The suffix of תּוֹכוֹ refers to

---

[24] Cf. G. Gerleman, *Ruth. Das Hohelied* (BKAT 18; Neukirchener Verlag: Neukirchen-Vluyn 1965) 139.

[25] Cf. M. Dahood, 'New Readings in Lamentations', *Bib* 59 (1978) 174-197:178 n.9. Dahood first emended to רָצוֹ, cf. id., *Proverbs*, 54.

[26] Cf. W. Kuhnigk, *Nordwestsemitische Studien zum Hoseabuch* (BibOr 27; Biblical Institute Press: Rome 1974) 20-21.

[27] Aartun, *UF* 10 (1978) 10-11.

מֶרְכָּבוֹ in v. 10a. Aartun denies that תּוֹכוֹ means 'interior'. It rather signifies 'middle,' and refers to the bride, not to the decoration of the litter. The predicate [רָצוּף] is derived from the root *רצף, 'to become hot, make hot'. The following preposition מִן expresses comparison, and the phrase מִבְּנוֹת יְרוּשָׁלָםִ is in apposition to the whole sentence. Hence, Aartun would translate 'whose centre (the centre of the seat of the litter) (is) made to glow, a love (more ardent) than (that) of the (amorous) daughters of Jerusalem'.[28] With regard to the translation of Dahood, Aartun asserts that

> the alleged syntactic combination of infinitive absolute ([רָצוֹ]) and an ordinary noun, and that by means of a particle (*pV*) which is otherwise foreign to the tradition of the Hebrew language, is even in common Semitic without analogy.

Dahood's proposal is therefore judged to be arbitrary.

The combination of infinitive absolute and ordinary noun linked by *waw* is, however, well attested in Biblical Hebrew. See Isa 32,17 וַעֲבֹדַת הַצְּדָקָה הַשְׁקֵט וָבֶטַח, 'the work of righteousness is quiet and security' where הַשְׁקֵט parses as hiphil infinitive absolute, while בֶטַח is an ordinary noun; Dan 1,17 נָתַן לָהֶם הָאֱלֹהִים מַדָּע וְהַשְׂכֵּל, 'God gave them knowledge and understanding' (הַשְׂכֵּל hiphil infinitive absolute); Lam 3,45 סְחִי וּמָאוֹס תְּשִׂימֵנוּ, 'you made us scum and refuse' (מָאוֹס qal infinitive absolute). Furthermore, according to the lexica, תּוֹכוֹ can signify, 'interior'.[29] The view that reference is being made to the bride rather than to the furnishing is interesting but

---

28 'dessen Mitte (die Mitte des Sitzes des Tragstuhls) (ist) glühend gemacht, eine Liebe (feuriger) als (die) der (liebenden) Töchter Jerusalems'.

29 Cf. *GesB*, 872b; *ZLH*, 891a; *HALAT*, 1564b.

does not impose itself.[30] In similar fashion Aartun's understanding of רָצוּף as signifying 'made to glow' is possible. The poet may have chosen the word for its diverse connotations. At least equally possible is its traditional association with the root meaning 'to arrange,' as favoured by Joüon who connects רָצוּף with the noun מַרְצֶפֶת which denotes an arrangement of objects, not necessarily of stone in the light of 2 Kgs 16,17 where אֲבָנִים, 'stones' is added to מַרְצֶפֶת.[31] In this context it suggests a work of embroidery. תּוֹכוֹ refers to the stitches of the embroidery (see Exod 39,3). אַהֲבָה מִבְּנוֹת יְרוּשָׁלָם he would take as in apposition to the preceding words. Hence, he renders, '(le siège est un tissu de pourpre,) brodé, gage d'amour des filles de Jérusalem'. Joüon does not render תּוֹכוֹ because he understands it as implied. It does seem a little strange, however, that when there are so few words in Hebrew, one should not be translated.

Pope parses תּוֹכוֹ as a noun, 'its interior' (of the litter), referring to the inlaid decoration.[32] He understands רָצוּף as 'pavement,' here designating decoration. The preposition מִן conceals in reality the enclitic *mem* which should be attached to אַהֲבָה, a word referring to the love scenes of the inlay.[33] בְּנוֹת יְרוּשָׁלַם then introduces the following verse. He translates, 'Its sides love inlaid'. Ravasi considers that אַהֲבָה is being employed adverbially, 'lovingly,'

---

30 Consult M.H. Pope, *Song of Songs*. A New Translation with Introduction and Commentary (AB7C; Doubleday: Garden City 1977) 444-445; L. Stadelmann, *Love and Politics*. A New Commentary on the Song of Songs (Paulist: New York 1992) 104; G. Ravasi, *Il Cantico dei cantici*. Commento e Attualizzazione (Testi e Commenti 4; Dehoniane: Bologna 1992) 326.

31 P. Joüon, *Le Cantique des Cantiques* (Beauchesne: Paris 1909) 189. Cf. *HALAT* 1198a s.v. רצף I.

32 Pope, *Song of Songs*, 444-446.

33 The preposition is parsed as partitive, literally 'some of the daughters' by Stadelmann, *Love and Politics*, 105.

and he translates, 'the interior inlaid lovingly by the daughters of Jerusalem'.[34] This apparently simple solution is not without difficulties. The adverbial force of אַהֲבָה is possible, as is the assumption that the daughters of Jerusalem made a kind of mosaic in stone, but elsewhere in the Song there is no reference to the daughters of Jerusalem making anything, and that they made a mosaic of stone does not seem probable. The other six instances of 'daughters of Jerusalem' in the Song are all vocative. Joüon more plausibly argues for something woven, but his explanation is complicated and does not appear to have won many adherents. It is precisely this uncertainty about the meaning of רָצוּף that led Dahood to make his suggestion which requires a rearrangement of the consonants and some revocalization but does yield obvious sense. No satisfactory explanation of the MT has yet been presented. Dahood's proposal which eliminates the hapaxlegomenon and attempts to elicit a straightforward meaning from the text remains worthy of consideration.

3. Hosea

אָלֹה וְכַחֵשׁ וְרָצֹחַ וְגָנֹב וְנָאֹף פָּרָצוּ וְדָמִים בְּדָמִים נָגָעוּ (Hos 4,2)

there is swearing, lying, killing, stealing, and committing adultery; they break all bounds and murder follows murder. (RSV)

Swearing and lying, and killing and stealing, and adultery and pleasure, and blood touches blood. (Dahood)[35]

---

[34] Ravasi, *Il Cantico dei cantici*, 303, 327 with reference to Joüon - Muraoka, *Grammar*, #102d. See the rendering of the RSV above.

[35] Dahood, *Proverbs*, 54; id., 'Ugaritic-Hebrew Parallel Pairs', *RSP* I, ch.2, nos. 171, 454; id., 'Ugaritic-Hebrew Parallel Pairs', *RSP* III, ch.1 Suppl. no. 89.

> Swearing (possibly false swearing) and lying and
> murdering and stealing and committing adultery.
> Break-ins are carried out, and blood guilt/bloody
> deeds follow blood guilt/bloody deeds. (Aartun)[36]

This is the only absolute use of the verb פרץ, and further, while it normally means 'to break through', it seems to requires here the sense of 'to be violent'. Some in consequence insert an object or prepositional phrase.[37] Dahood would retain the consonantal text but read פְּרָצוֹ, parsing the vocable as the conjunction פ and the infinitive absolute רָצוֹ from רָצָה, 'be pleased'. He explains

> This analysis would account for the apparent lack of a conjunction between [נָאֹף] and [פרזו], and further obviates the need for determining what [פָּרַץ] denotes in this context'.

One may add that the resulting balance in the pairs of nouns helps to make Dahood's proposal attractive.

Aartun denies that the infinitive forms may be subject of the following verbs and points out that an infinitive absolute without qualification functions adverbially in Hebrew. The free-standing infinitives simply express the verbal concept. He sees no difficulty with the meaning of the verb. The reasons that move commentators to make changes in the text are, however, not considered. Aartun's own translation is not without difficulty. פרץ in the sense of 'break

---

[36] 'Verfluchen (eventuell falsch schwören) und Lügen und Morden und Stehlen und Ehebrechen! Man macht Einbruch, und Blutschuld/Bluttat reiht sich an Blutschuld/Bluttat'. Cf. Aartun, 'Textüberlieferung', *UF* 10 (1978) 12.

[37] Cf. H.W. Wolff, *Dodekapropheton I: Hosea* (BKAT 14/1; Neukirchener Verlag: Neukirchen-Vluyn [2]1965) 81 (E.V. 65); D. Stuart, *Hosea-Jonah* (WBC 31; Waco: Word Books 1987) 72: 'restoring בארץ with G'. See *BHS*.

into' is elsewhere found only with an accusative which is lacking in Hos 4,2. See 2 Chr 24,7 פָּרְצוּ אֶת־בֵּית הָאֱלֹהִים, '(they) broke into (down?) the house of God'.[38] Furthermore, 'stealing' has just been mentioned. Hence, it is unlikely that פרץ carries this meaning here. Kuhnigk expresses doubts about Dahood's suggestion in the light of Jer 7,9 and Exod 20,13-16 (Deut 5,17-20).[39] But the similarities between these texts do not really prove anything about Hos 4,2 which is cast in poetic form. The weight to be given Dahood's proposal depends in part on the importance attached to the difficulty of the text. Most commentators do in fact find it awkward. Hence, Dahood's proposal cannot be simply dismissed as improbable.

> וְגַנָּב יָבוֹא פָּשַׁט גְּדוּד בַּחוּץ (Hos 7,1b)
>
> The thief breaks in, and the bandits raid without. (RSV)
>
> The thief shall come and the marauding band shall roam the streets. (Dahood)[40]
>
> A gang of thieves will come,
> A gang of thieves will mug (people) in the streets. (Andersen and Freedman)[41]
>
> *καὶ κλέπτης πρὸς αὐτὸν εἰσελεύσεται* (LXX)
> And the thief shall come in to him.

While the Vulgate supports the Massoretic tradition, the LXX gives the verb a complement. Commentators frequently remark on the lack

---

[38] Consult *BDB*, 829a; *HALAT*, 914b.

[39] Cf. Kuhnigk, *Hoseabuch*, 26 n.87.

[40] Dahood, *Proverbs*, 54; id., 'The Conjunction *pa* in Hosea 7,1,' *Bib* 57 (1976) 247-248.

[41] F.I. Andersen - D.N. Freedman, *Hosea*. Introduction, Translation, and Notes (AB 24; Doubleday: Garden City 1980) 432.

of complement for יָבוֹא and either insert a phrase[42] or like the RSV add 'and' in the translation.[43] It is true that בוא is often found without a complement, but here the parallelism makes its presence desirable. וְגַנָּב יָבוֹא is parallel to גְּדוּד פָּשַׁט, but there is nothing in the first part of the line to balance בַּחוּץ. Dahood tries to solve the problem by analysing פָּשַׁט as the conjunction פ plus שָׁט from שׁוּט, 'to roam, range'. This provides a complement for יָבוֹא and effects good parallelism between the two verbs. Dahood also notes their collocation in Job 1,7 and 2,2.[44]

Aartun analyses the second half of the line as an asyndetic verbal clause but sees no problem in the text.[45] The reading of the LXX represents a secondary variant. He translates, 'and the thief enters by force (literally: comes)' which 'is parallel to' 'the band outside has set out'.[46] Nevertheless, such a translation does some violence to the text. 'Enters by force' hardly represents יָבוֹא, nor is 'has set out' a very satisfactory rendering of פָּשַׁט which includes the sense of 'raiding'. The parallel is not exact.

Andersen and Freedman point out that the lack of a coordinating conjunction is typical of Hosea but do not consider the matter of a complement for יָבוֹא.[47] Dahood's analysis implies a considerable grammatical change in the traditional understanding of פָּשַׁט. On the other hand, unlike a number of other proposals, this one

---

[42] Cf. W.R. Harper, *A Critical and Exegetical Commentary on Amos and Hosea* (ICC; T. & T. Clark: Edinburgh 1904) 291: 'add בַּיְתָה'; A. van Hoonacker, *Les Douze Petits Prophètes* (Gabalda: Paris 1908) 68: the LXX suggests עָלֶיהָ.

[43] Cf. Wolff, *Hosea*, 135 (E.V. 106).

[44] Dahood, 'The Conjunction *pa*', *Bib* 57 (1976) 247.

[45] Aartun, 'Textüberlieferung', *UF* 10 (1978) 13.

[46] 'und der Dieb dringt ein (wörtlich: kommt)'...'es ist die Bande draußen losgezogen'.

[47] Andersen and Freedman, *Hosea*, 445.

requires only a small modification of the MT.[48] It makes good sense and looks plausible.[49]

When introducing the inquiry, Aartun lays emphasis on the importance of the relationship between the oral and written tradition of the text. Where the ketib and qere agree he would be most reluctant to allow a change.[50] Dahood on the other hand believed that an entirely new approach was necessary, one that took into account not only the earlier tradition of the language but also related languages and dialects. He judged that the later tradition was no very reliable guide to the text and not infrequently misunderstood it.[51] The present study has not treated these important points of methodology, though they are likely to influence conclusions. The proposed instances of the particle פ have been judged plausible or otherwise on their grammatical merits. Since no grammatical reason has been advanced for Job 16,14, the presence of פ, 'and' here would appear problematic. On the other hand, the particle may very probably be found in Ps 50,10. Its presence in Cant 3,10; Hos 4,2; 7,1 can be considered probable. Granted the existence of the particle in Biblical Hebrew, Job 9,12.20 will make more sense.

---

48 Dahood vocalizes פְּ.

49 See Kuhnigk, *Hoseabuch*, 87-88; Stuart, *Hosea-Jonah*, 116, 'The MT consonantal text may be read either פָּשַׁט or פְּשָׁט, the latter being the conjunction, "and" + the ptcp of שׁוּט'.

50 Aartun, 'Textüberlieferung', *UF* 10 (1978) 2-3.

51 See for instance Dahood, 'Northwest Semitic Texts', BETL 33, 11-19.

6
Misunderstood Vocative Particles

In this chapter we shall treat three clitics with emphatic functions: *l*-, *k*- and *mem*. The particular nuance of the 'emphasis' is vocative, that is an appeal to the intended interlocutor or hearer. These three clitics actually have different origins. Only *l*- (vocalised in Hebrew as the preposition *l*-) is originally an emphatic particle.[1] *k*- is a deictic particle. It grammaticalises the intention of the speaker to identify certain things in the real world (as opposed to linguistic realities) as relevant. Hence, it is employed for comparison (preposition *k*-), for coordinating in time (*kî* 'when'), for eliciting a reason or motivation (*kî* 'because'), *kōh* 'thus'. In a certain environment this deictic *kî*, in whatever form it may appear in the MT, produces the same effect as our way of calling attention to our intended interlocutors. *mî* with a vocative function is attested in the formula *mî yittēn*, 'O that'. In Ugaritic *my* can serve the same function. Thus KTU 1.5(67).VI:23-25

> *my.lim.bn (24) dgn.my.hmlt.aṯr (25) bʿl.ard b arṣ*
>
> O mankind, sons of Dagan, O multitude!
> I wish I could go down to the underworld in Baal's place.

[1] See F. Nötscher, 'Zum emphatischen Lamed', *VT* 3 (1953) 372-380.

The interrogative pronoun *my*, literally 'who' here expresses a certain exasperation directed at *lim* and *hmlt*. We perceive this as vocative. The same can be said of *mî yittēn*, 'O that...' 'who will grant me'. Ugaritic and Hebrew have conventionalised this expression of exasperation directed at particular addressees with *mî*.

1. Vocative *kî*

M. Dahood put forward the hypothesis that a number of passages in the Hebrew Bible could be rendered more easily if כִּי (כ) were parsed as a vocative particle. The suggestion appears to have been made in only two articles published during the 1970s, one in a *Festschrift* and the other in a review of a dictionary.[2] It is therefore not unlikely that many are unaware of the proposal. A reconsideration of the arguments in favour of the particle's existence in Biblical Hebrew may therefore be appropriate.[3]

---

[2] M. Dahood, 'Vocative *kî* and *wa* in Biblical Hebrew,' *Mélanges offerts au R.P. Henri Fleisch, S.J.* (*Mélanges de l'Université Saint-Joseph* 48 [1973-1974]) 49-63, esp. 49-59; id., 'Hebrew Lexicography: A Review of W. Baumgartner's *Lexikon*, Volume II,' *Or* n.s. 45 (1976) 327-365, esp. 328-329, 338 where it is suggested the particle may also appear in Ugaritic. Dahood proposed UT 49.IV:25-27 (KTU 1.6:IV:1-3) *pl ʿnt šdm y špš / pl ʿnt šdm il yštk /* bʿ*l ʿnt mḥrṯt*, 'Fissured the furrows of the fields, O Shapsh / fissured the furrows of the fields, El / dried up (root *nšt*), O Baal, are the furrows of the plowland!'; ʿnt.III:5-7 (KTU 1.3.III:8-10) *km ǵlmm / w.ʿrbn.lpʿn.ʿnt.*hbr */ w ql*, 'O youths and entrants / at Anath's feet bow and fall!'. The suggestion does not seem to have won adherents.

[3] Dahood considers the vocative כִּי to be related to or identical with the emphatic כִּי, cf. id., 'Vocative *kî* and *wa*', *Mélanges*, 51-52. On the emphatic כִּי, see the discussions in J. Muilenburg, 'The Linguistic and Rhetorical Usages of the Particle כי in the Old Testament,' *HUCA* 32 (1961) 135-160; A. Schoors, 'The Particle כי,' *OTS* 21 (1981) 240-276, esp. 243-253; W.T. Claassen, 'Speaker-Orientated Functions of *kî* in Biblical Hebrew,' *JNSL* 11 (1983) 29-46; T. Muraoka, *Emphatic Words and Structures in Biblical Hebrew* (Magnes: Jerusalem 1985) 158-164; A. Aejmelaeus, 'Function and Interpretation of כי in Biblical Hebrew,' *JBL* 105 (1986) 193-209. Dahood finds numerous examples, cf. Martinez, *Index* I, 117; II, 127; Dahood, *Psalms* III, 402-406.

וְאַתָּה הָשְׁלַכְתָּ מִקִּבְרְךָ כְּנֵצֶר נִתְעָב
לְבוּשׁ הֲרֻגִים מְטֹעֲנֵי חָרֶב
יוֹרְדֵי אֶל־אַבְנֵי־בוֹר כְּפֶגֶר מוּבָס (Isa 14,19)

but you are cast out, away from your sepulchre, like a loathed untimely birth, clothed with the slain, those pierced by the sword, who go down to the stones of the Pit, like a dead body trodden under foot. (RSV)

But you have been tossed from your tomb, O loathsome offshoot! covered by the slain pierced by the sword, who have gone down to the stones of the Pit, O trampled corpse! (Dahood)[4]

The RSV follows Simmachus and the Targum in reading נפל (εκτρωμα) for the Massoretic נצר. Wildberger who favours the same emendation argues that no one will ask whether a shoot is to be buried.[5] To obviate this difficulty Dahood revocalises *kīnēṣer* (MT *kᵉnēṣer*), 'O (loathsome) offshoot,' parsing *kī* as vocative *kî* and drawing attention to the metaphorical use of *nēṣer* in Isa 11,1. In the same way he alters *kᵉpeger* to *kīpeger*, and renders 'O (trampled) corpse'. This proposal makes good sense and requires only slight changes in the vocalisation of the text.[6] It is well known that the

---

[4] Dahood, 'Vocative *kî* and *wa*', *Mélanges*, 53.

[5] H. Wildberger, *Jesaja*. 2. Teilband. *Jesaja 13-27* (BKAT 10/2; Neukirchener Verlag: Neukirchen-Vluyn 1978) 536. The emendation is made by the NRSV, REB and J.D.W. Watts, *Isaiah 1-33* (WBC 24; Waco: Word Books, 1985) 207. The NAB reads כְּנֵצֶל, rendering 'corrupt'. See the discussion in G.B. Gray, *A Critical and Exegetical Commentary on the Book of Isaiah I-XXVII* (ICC; T. & T. Clark: Edinburgh 1912) 259.

[6] The retention of כְּנֵצֶר may also be supported by formal considerations, cf. R.H. O'Connell, 'Isaiah xiv 4b-23: Ironic Reversal through Concentric Structure and Mythic Allusion,' *VT* 38 (1988) 407-418. O'Connell argues that 'You are...like a rejected branch' balances v. 8, with both verses employing plant imagery, see esp. pp. 408, 412.

particle *kî* fulfils a variety of functions and Dahood's suggestion avoids the emendations commonly practised. It seems to offer a plausible explanation of the text.

מַשָּׂא מוֹאָב
כִּי בְּלֵיל שֻׁדַּד עָר מוֹאָב נִדְמָה
כִּי בְּלֵיל שֻׁדַּד קִיר־מוֹאָב נִדְמָה (Isa 15,1)
An oracle concerning Moab.
Because Ar is laid waste in a night
Moab is undone;
because Kir is laid waste in a night
Moab is undone. (RSV)

O devastated in a night,
Guardian of Moab laid waste!
O devastated in a night,
Kir of Moab laid waste! (Dahood)[7]

The RSV's stichometry which separates קִיר from מוֹאָב differs from that of the Massoretes but may be preferable in view of the parallelism. The name קִיר־מוֹאָב does not occur elsewhere. Less obvious is the translation of the first כִּי with 'Because'. At the beginning of an oracle an assertion is expected, not a reason. It is doubtless for this reason that the LXX and many modern versions offer no translation of כִּי.[8] The Vulgate renders, 'autem'. The oracle is the first of a series and it is worth noting that the next מַשָּׂא in 17,1 opens with הִנֵּה, as does that in 19,1, while the oracle in 18,1 (lacking מַשָּׂא) commences with הוֹי. Some commentators therefore understand

---

[7] Dahood, 'Vocative *kî* and *wa*', *Mélanges*, 53.
[8] Cf. NEB, NAB, NIV, REB.

the particle in our oracle to be asseverative.[9] Dahood proposes to explain כִּי as a vocative. The next address is in 16,1 which apparently carries on the oracle, and the second person continues till 16,4. The variation between second and third person is common in Hebrew poetry so that it would not astonish if a second person in 15,1 were replaced by a third person in the following verses only to emerge again in 16,1. A vocative makes good sense in 15,1.

הוֹי אֲרִיאֵל אֲרִיאֵל קִרְיַת חָנָה דָוִד סְפוּ שָׁנָה עַל־שָׁנָה
חַגִּים יִנְקֹפוּ׃
וַהֲצִיקוֹתִי לַאֲרִיאֵל וְהָיְתָה תַאֲנִיָּה וַאֲנִיָּה
וְהָיְתָה לִּי כַּאֲרִיאֵל׃
וְחָנִיתִי כַדּוּר עָלָיִךְ (Isa 29,1-3)

v.1 Ho Ariel, Ariel, the city where David encamped!
Add year to year; let the feasts run their round.
v.2 Yet I will distress Ariel,
and there shall be moaning and lamentation,
and she shall be to me like an Ariel.
v.3 And I will encamp against you round about. (RSV)

v.2 And I will close in, O Ariel,
and there will be moaning and lamentation;
you will be mine, O Ariel,
v.3 and I will encamp before you, O Village. (Dahood)[10]

---

[9] Watts (*Isaiah* 1-33, 233) renders 'Indeed!' and Wildberger (*Jesaja* 2, 588) 'Wahrlich'. Clements judges the particle to be asseverative on the grounds that this removes the need for supposing the omission of a preceding clause. Cf. R.E. Clements, *Isaiah 1-39* (NCBC; Marshall, Morgan and Scott: London 1980) 151. It is possible that the causal clause may simply be prefixed (see Gray, *Isaiah*, 280-281), but, as has been seen, the wider context does not seem to support this view.

[10] Dahood, 'Vocative *kî* and *wa*', *Mêlanges*, 54.

Dahood points to the shift of person in these verses. To avoid it he parses לַאֲרִיאֵל (v. 2) as vocative. In similar fashion he takes the next occurrence of 'Ariel' as vocative, reading כְּאֲרִיאֵל (MT כַּאֲרִיאֵל) and וְהָיִיתָה (MT וְהָיְתָה), 'you will be mine, O Ariel'.[11] אֲרִיאֵל is often related to וְהַהַרְאֵל and וְהָאֲרִאֵיל (qere והאריאל) in Ezek 43,15.16, which signify 'altar of burnt-sacrifice'.[12] This is no doubt connoted by 'Ariel' in Isaiah 29. The words are not identical but the alliteration and assonance are so striking that a play on words resulted. In any case the primary reference is to Jerusalem, and the vocative is therefore appropriate.

In v. 3a כַדּוּר is generally related to דּוֹר 'circle' and understood in the sense of the RSV, though some would emend to כְּדָוִד 'like David' in the light of ὡς Δαυιδ by the LXX.[13] Relevant is דּוֹרִי in Isa 38,12, which *HALAT* understands as 'tent camp', 'place of residence' in the light of the Aramaic דּוּרָא.[14] Dahood would interpret כדור in Isaiah 29 after the same fashion. He reads כְּדוּר parsed as the vocative כְּ followed by the noun דור understood to signify 'village', and the counterpart of קִרְיַת in v. 1, 'And I will encamp before you, O village'. This produces a tauter line and effects a balance with the second stich. Though attractive the proposal must remain

---

[11] See *1QIsa*[a] והייתה (Burrows, *The Dead Sea Scrolls of St. Mark's Monastery*, pl. xxiii). The emendation to 2 f.s. וְהָיִת was proposed by B. Duhm, *Das Buch Jesaia* (Vandenhoeck & Ruprecht: Göttingen 1914) 181; cf. H. Wildberger, *Jesaja* 3. Teilband *Jesaja 28-39*. Das Buch, der Prophet und seine Botschaft (BKAT 10/3; Neukirchener Verlag: Neukirchen-Vluyn 1984) 1098; Clements, *Isaiah 1-39*, 236; *BHS*.

[12] Cf. Wildberger, *Jesaja* 3, 1098; Clements, *Isaiah 1-39*, 235; Watts, *Isaiah*, 378.

[13] So *BHS*.

[14] Cf. *HALAT*, 209a s.v. I דּוֹר 'Zeltlager, Wohnstatt'; W.H. Irwin, *Isaiah 28-33 Translation with Philological Notes* (BibOr 30; Biblical Institute Press: Rome 1977) 49.

hypothetical in view of the uncertainty surrounding the meaning of the noun.

> כִּי־עַם בְּצִיּוֹן יֵשֵׁב בִּירוּשָׁלִָם
> בָּכוֹ לֹא־תִבְכֶּה
> חָנוֹן יָחְנְךָ לְקוֹל זַעֲקֶךָ
> כְּשָׁמְעָתוֹ עָנָךְ (Isa 30,19)
>
> Yea, O people in Zion who dwell at Jerusalem; you shall weep no more. He will surely be gracious to you at the sound of your cry; when he hears it, he will answer you. (RSV)
>
> O people dwelling in Zion,
> in Jerusalem you shall weep no more;
> he will be most gracious to you at the sound of your cry;
> when he hears he will answer you. (Dahood)[15]

The RSV sets out the text as prose, but *BHS* prints it as poetry and Dahood concurs.[16] The matter is important. Clements would delete 'in Zion' as superfluous beside 'at Jerusalem'.[17] Wildberger favours the same deletion on the grounds that the first hemistich is overloaded.[18] The overloading is true in view of his stichometry, for he includes בירושלם in the first stich, placing only בָּכוֹ לֹא־תִבְכֶּה in the second. A balanced arrangement of the text without deletion is

[15] Dahood, 'Vocative *kî* and *wa*', *Mélanges*, 52.

[16] NIV, NRSV, REB, Watts, *Isaiah*, 398 and E.I. Young, *The Book of Isaiah*. The English Text, with Introduction, Exposition, and Notes: Chapters 1-18 (Eerdmans: Grand Rapids ²1972) 354 set out the verse as prose, NAB, NJB and Wildberger, *Jesaja* 3, 1189 as poetry.

[17] Clements, *Isaiah*, 250.

[18] Wildberger, *Jesaia* 3, 1190.

proposed by Dahood and set out above.[19] He observes that there is chiasmus in the first two stichs, the sequence being subject-prepositional phrase-prepositional phrase-subject, arguing further that since תִבְכֶּה is second person, its subject עַם should accordingly be the addressee. He therefore interprets the emphatic nuance of כִּי as vocative.

Dahood revocalises the finite verb יֵשֵׁב as participle יֹשֵׁב, and translates 'O people dwelling in Zion'.[20] The emendation enjoys some support among ancient authorities, for the Syriac reads *yāteb*, the Targum יתיב, although it is probable that both versions employed the more usual construction to facilitate the translation. The alteration may not be necessary. Irwin notes that בִּירוּשָׁלַםִיֵשֵׁב can be explained as an asyndetic relative clause, functioning as a vocative.[21]

Dahood further observes that vocative כִּי is primarily a poetic particle and he draws attention to poetic features in the passage. The scansion is 3+3+2+2+2, the two infinitives absolute in the second and third stichs have an intensifying function, while temporal לְ in לְקוֹל and temporal כְּ in כְּשָׁמְעָתוֹ show stylistic variation. One may add that there is also chiasmus in the second half of the verse. עָנָךְ balances חָנוֹן יָחְנְךָ while כְּשָׁמְעָתוֹ responds to לְקוֹל זַעֲקֶךָ. At the same time לְקוֹל זַעֲקֶךָ functions as a pivot between the preceding stich and the following one. It would appear that Dahood has made out a plausible argument both for the poetic character of the verse and for the parsing of כִּי as vocative.

עוּרִי עוּרִי לִבְשִׁי עֻזֵּךְ צִיּוֹן (Isa 52,1)

---

[19] It is also possible to take the verse up to תִבְכֶּה as three stichs, 'O people in Zion, you who dwell in Jerusalem, you shall not weep any more!' Cf. Irwin, *Isaiah*, 88.

[20] This emendation is commonly made, see for instance Wildberger, *Jesaja* 3, 1190.

[21] Irwin, *Isaiah*, 56. See Isa 29,9 and Ehrlich, *Randglossen* IV, 104.

Awake, awake, put on your strength,
O Zion. (RSV)

עורי עורי לבשי עוז ציון (*1QIsa*[a])[22]
Awake, awake, put on strength, Zion.

The translation of the RSV is unexceptionable, but Dahood draws attention to the variant in *1QIsa*[a] which omits the suffix of MT עֻזֵּךְ, 'your strength'.[23] He argues that *1QIsa*[a] was apparently influenced by Isa 51,9 עוּרִי עוּרִי לִבְשִׁי־עֹז זְרוֹעַ יְהוָה 'Awake, awake, put on strength, O arm of the Lord' where עֹז also lacks the suffix. Dahood proposes to understand the suffix ךְ- in Isa 52,1 as the vocative particle and so scans

עוּרִי עוּרִי לִבְשִׁי עֹז כִּ צִיּוֹן
Awake, awake, put on strength, O Zion!

He explains

> By adding another beat, the new reading gives greater substance to the second colon and improves the stichometry; the line now reads as three plus two, precisely like Isa 51,9.

The RSV supposes a 2+3 beat, but the oracle in 52,1-2 contains no other example of a line in which the first stich has fewer beats than the second. *BHS* scans 3+2 but at the price of enjambement and against the manuscript accentuation which links לִבְשִׁי and עֹז. Dahood's suggestion would appear metrically preferable to both the

22 See Burrows, *The Dead Sea Scrolls of St. Mark's Monastery*, pl. xliii.
23 Dahood, 'Vocative *kî* and *wa*', *Mêlanges*, 51.

RSV and *BHS*. In the light of Isa 51,9 the proposal is not implausible.

> כִּי מִי־יַחְמֹל עָלַיִךְ יְרוּשָׁלַםִ
> וּמִי יָנוּד לָךְ (Jer 15,5)
> Who will have pity on you, O Jerusalem,
> or who will bemoan you? (RSV)
>
> O who will take pity on you, Jerusalem,
> and who will lament for you? (Dahood)[24]

It can be seen that the RSV fails to render the initial כִּי, following the example of the LXX and the Syriac and in line with most modern translations.[25] McKane judges the particle to be a redactional link, apparently following the view of Ziegler and Janzen who argue that it is a Massoretic conflation.[26] Holladay considers it to be an emphatic particle, 'So who will pity you, Jerusalem?'[27] Dahood more precisely

---

24 Dahood, 'Vocative *kî* and *wa*', *Mêlanges*, 55.

25 J. Bright, *Jeremiah*. Introduction, Translation, and Notes (AB 21; Doubleday: Garden City 1965) 105; J.A. Thompson, *The Book of Jeremiah* (NICOT; Eerdmans: Grand Rapids 1980) 388; R.P. Carroll, *Jeremiah*. A Commentary (OTL; SCM: London 1986) 321; NAB, NJB, REB, NRSV.

26 W. McKane, *A Critical and Exegetical Commentary on Jeremiah*. Introduction and Commentary on Jeremiah I-XXV (ICC; T. T. Clark: Edinburgh 1986) 337; J. Ziegler, *Beiträge zur Jeremias-Septuaginta* (Vandenhoeck & Ruprecht: Göttingen 1958) 87; J.G. Janzen, *Studies in the Text of Jeremiah* (HSM 6; Harvard University Press: Cambridge 1973) 25.

27 W.L. Holladay, *Jeremiah*. A Commentary on the Book of the Prophet Jeremiah Chapters 1-25 (Hermeneia; Fortress: Philadelphia 1986) 421, 441. So already G. del Olmo Lete, 'Notas críticas al texto hebreo de Jr. 14-17,' *Claretianum* 11 (1971) 316; W.A.M. Beuken - H.W.M. van Grol, 'Jeremiah 14,1-15,9: A Situation of Distress and its Hermeneutics. Unity and Diversity of Form - Dramatic Development,' *Le Livre de Jérêmie*. Le prophète et son milieu. Les oracles et leur transmission (ed. P.-M. Bogaert) (BETL 54; Peeters: Leuven 1981) 307.

sees here an expression of pain and longing. This would bring out the meaning best.

> כִּי אָז תֵּבֹשִׁי וְנִכְלַמְתְּ מִכֹּל רָעָתֵךְ (Jer 22,22b)
> then you will be ashamed and confounded
> because of all your wickedness. (RSV)
>
> O then you will be ashamed and abashed
> for all your evildoing. (Dahood)[28]

The RSV again fails to translate כִּי.[29] The NAB renders, 'Surely'.[30] Bright catches the note of lament with, 'Ah, but then...'[31] He and Dahood both recognise the particular nuance possessed by כִּי in the context.

> אַל־תִּשְׂמַח יִשְׂרָאֵל אֶל־גִּיל כָּעַמִּים (Hos 9,1)
> Rejoice not, O Israel!
> Exult not like the peoples. (RSV)
>
> Do not rejoice, Israel,
> let there be no joy, O peoples! (Dahood)[32]

The parallelism between the two stichs supports the RSV's interpretation of אֶל־גִּיל as negative.[33] Dahood reads כְּעַמִּים for the Massoretes' כָּעַמִּים, arguing that

---

[28] Dahood, 'Vocative *kî* and *wa*', *Mélanges*, 55.

[29] So too NRSV, NJB, REB, Carroll, *Jeremiah*, 434; McKane, *Jeremiah* I, 534.

[30] Holladay, *Jeremiah*. Chapters 1-25, 600: 'Yes'.

[31] Bright, *Jeremiah*, 138.

[32] Dahood, 'Vocative *kî* and *wa*', *Mélanges*, 56.

[33] It may not be necessary to emend the text from אֶל to אַל, cf. F.I. Andersen - D.N. Freedman, *Hosea*. Introduction, Translation, and Notes (AB 24; Doubleday: Garden City 1980) 522.

> Since the pagans would naturally exult over Israel's apostasy from Yahweh, they are warned along with Israel not to take satisfaction from such a decline of religious ideals.

This is interesting exegesis, but despite the improved parallelism the vocative does not impose itself.

> אוֹדְךָ לְעוֹלָם כִּי עָשִׂיתָ וַאֲקַוֶּה שִׁמְךָ כִי־טוֹב
> נֶגֶד חֲסִידֶיךָ (Ps 52,11)
> I will thank thee for ever, because thou hast done it.
> I will proclaim thy name, for it is good,
> in the presence of the godly. (RSV)
>
> I will praise you, O Eternal, because you acted;
> And I will proclaim your name, O Good One,
> before your devoted servants. (Dahood)[34]

Dahood interprets both לְעוֹלָם and כִי־טוֹב as divine titles in the vocative, 'O Eternal,' 'O Good One'. Leaving aside לְעוֹלָם, the expression כִי־טוֹב occurs not infrequently and its meaning has been much discussed. Dahood's proposal is possible, especially if his translation of the first stich is accepted, but the traditional understanding of the phrase can be retained.[35]

> בִּנְדָבָה אֶזְבְּחָה־לָּךְ אוֹדֶה שִּׁמְךָ יְהוָה כִּי־טוֹב (Ps 54,8)
> With a freewill offering I will sacrifice to thee;
> I will give thanks to thy name, O LORD, for it is good. (RSV)

---

[34] Dahood, 'Vocative *kî* and *wa*', *Mélanges*, 57.

[35] Cf. A. Schoors, 'The Particle כי,' *OTS* 21 (1981) 273-275.

v.8b I will praise your Name Yahweh,
O Good One. (Dahood)[36]

The RSV is representative of modern versions when it scans the verse as a bicolon with a 2:4 metre, but this does not look right. No other verse in the psalm has more beats in the second parallel stich, and Kraus senses this difficulty when he deletes יהוה *metri causa*.[37] Dahood points out that v. 8b scans as a bicolon with a 5:4 syllable count when כִּי is parsed as vocative. This is much more satisfactory metrically.

אוֹדְךָ בָעַמִּים אֲדֹנָי אֲזַמֶּרְךָ בַּל־אֻמִּים׃
כִּי־גָדֹל עַד־שָׁמַיִם חַסְדֶּךָ
וְעַד־שְׁחָקִים אֲמִתֶּךָ (Ps 57,10-11 (=Ps 108,4-5)
I will give thanks to thee, O Lord, among the peoples;
I will sing praises to thee among the nations.
For thy steadfast love is great to the heavens,
thy faithfulness to the clouds. (RSV)

I will thank you among peoples, Lord,
I will sing to [you] among nations, O Great One!
To the heavens your kindness,
yes, to the sky your fidelity. (Dahood)[38]

Dahood takes כִּי־גָדֹל with the end of v. 10, understanding the particle as vocative. He argues that this analysis yields greater symmetry. The two vocatives in v. 10 are parallel, while in v. 11 the two

---

[36] Dahood, *Psalms* II, 23, 27; id., 'Vocative *kî* and *wa*', *Mélanges*, 57.

[37] H.-J. Kraus, *Psalmen* 1. Teilband: *Psalmen 1-59* (BKAT 15/1; Neukirchen-Vluyn: Neukirchener Verlag, [5]1978) 555.

[38] Dahood, 'Vocative *kî* and *wa*', *Mélanges*, 57.

nominal clauses are perfectly balanced. V. 10 now has 3+3 beats, v. 11 2+2. Though there is no grammatical difficulty so that the ordinary understanding of the verse is acceptable, this is an attractive proposal from a prosodic viewpoint.

> וְאַתָּה יְהוִה אֲדֹנָי עֲשֵׂה־אִתִּי לְמַעַן שְׁמֶךָ
> כִּי־טוֹב חַסְדְּךָ הַצִּילֵנִי (Ps 109,21)
> But thou, O GOD my Lord,
> deal on my behalf for thy name's sake;
> because thy steadfast love is good, deliver me! (RSV)
>
> (But thou, O GOD my Lord,)
> Work a miracle for me
> for the sake of your Name, O Good One. (Dahood)[39]

The RSV takes טוֹב to be an adjective, which is how the Massoretes understood it. It is also possible to parse טוֹב as a noun, following the Syriac and the Targum which read כטוב.[40] Michael L. Barré has argued strongly in favour of this change to the MT on the grounds that טוֹב and חֶסֶד are a fixed formulaic pair and should be understood as a hendiadys which can be translated, 'according to your steadfast goodness'.[41] Dahood also parses טוֹב as a noun, but interpreted as a divine appellative, 'Good One,' כִּי then being the vocative particle. To avoid an overlong stich he takes חַסְדְּךָ הַצִּילֵנִי with the next verse and scans: עֲשֵׂה־אִתִּי לְמַעַן שְׁמֶךָ כִּי־טוֹב, 'work a miracle for me / for

---

39 Dahood, 'Hebrew Lexicography,' *Or* n.s. 45 (1976) 328-329, reading אֹתִי for MT אִתִּי.

40 E.g. H.-J. Kraus, *Psalmen* 2. Teilband: *Psalmen 60-150* (BKAT 15/2; Neukirchener Verlag: Neukirchen-Vluyn ^{5}1978) 919 n.p.

41 M.L. Barré, 'The Formulaic Pair טוב (ו)חסד in the Psalter,' *ZAW* 98 (1986) 100-105.

the sake of your Name, O Good One'. Leaving aside Dahood's emendation of the MT, his reading runs counter to the position of Barré that טוֹב and חֶסֶד represent a fixed pair. While Barré's evidence is not without weight it cannot demonstrate that in this particular instance the hendiadys is necessarily present, for the tradition handed down by the Massoretes apparently read כִּי rather than כ.[42] Dahood's proposal is attractive to the extent that it explains the text and offers a reasonable stichometry.

חָנֵּנוּ יְהוָה חָנֵּנוּ כִּי־רַב שָׂבַעְנוּ בוּז (Ps 123,3)
Have mercy upon us, O LORD, have mercy upon us,
for we have had more than enough of contempt. (RSV)

Have pity on us, Yahweh,
Have pity on us, O Master,
we are sated with contempt. (Dahood)[43]

Kraus notes that the predominant metre in the psalm is 3+2 and in consequence finds v. 3b overloaded, so that he deletes רַב.[44] Dahood proposes taking רַב as a noun, 'master' preceded by the vocative כִּי. He scans the verse as three stichs. Here too the parallel vocatives permit a more convincing stichometry with a 5:5:4 syllable pattern.[45] It is true that רַב is not generally recognised as being a divine title, since it normally designates foreigners, but in this psalm the proposal makes good sense and solves the metrical difficulty. The poetic

---

[42] *11QPs*[a] also reads כי. Cf. J.A. Sanders, *The Psalms Scroll of Qumrân Cave 11* (DJD 4; Clarendon: Oxford 1965) pl. 3.

[43] Dahood, 'Vocative *kî* and *wa*', *Mélanges*, 58.

[44] Cf. Kraus, *Psalmen* II, 1021; *BHS*.

[45] Cf. Dahood, *Psalms* III, 209.

nuance of the word כִּי also seems more appropriate than the prosaic 'for'.

In conclusion we suggest that the following examples of the vocative כִּי offer a considerable measure of plausibility: Isa 14,19: to avoid substantial emendation; 30,19: avoids emendation; Jer 15,5 and 22,22b: explains כִּי. In the following passages the stichometry is improved, but the traditional understanding remains quite possible: Pss 54,8; 57,10-11; 109,21; 123,3.

2. Vocative *lamed*

Patrick D. Miller precedes his investigation of the vocative *lamed* in the Psalter with an examination of 32 examples in Ugaritic. He concludes that this particle is common in Ugaritic, being used most frequently with imperative verbs and nearly always immediately after them. The basic presupposition shared by Miller and Dahood is that there are affinities between Ugaritic and Biblical Hebrew. Yet, whereas Dahood claimed many examples of the particle for Biblical Hebrew, Miller remained skeptical. The question of whether the vocative *lamed* should be accepted in Hebrew grammars has been answered in different ways. While some like Miller have expressed doubts about its existence in the language,[46] others would admit several examples.[47] Waltke and O'Connor include the vocative *lamed* in their grammar.[48] In view of Miller's careful study of the instances

[46] Cf. P.D. Miller, 'Vocative Lamed in the Psalter: A Reconsideration,' *UF* 11 (1979) 617-637; J. Huehnergard, 'Asseverative **la* and Hypothetical **lu/law* in Semitic,' *JAOS* 103 (1983) 569-593, esp. 591.

[47] M. Dahood has proposed numerous examples, cf. id., *Psalms* III, 407-408; Martinez, *Index* I, 117 and II, 128. See too T. Penar, '"Lamedh Vocativi" exempla biblico-hebraica,' *Verbum Domini* 45 (1967) 32-46; *HALAT* 485b-486; M.H. Pope, 'Vestiges of Vocative *lamedh* in the Bible,' *UF* 20 (1988) 201-207.

[48] *WOC*, #11.2.10i (pp. 211-212).

alleged for the Psalter, it does not appear useful to consider all these cases again. Nonetheless, it may be appropriate to take another look at those occurrences deemed by him and others to have a measure of probability.

קוּמָה יְהוָה הוֹשִׁיעֵנִי אֱלֹהַי
כִּי־הִכִּיתָ אֶת־כָּל־אֹיְבַי לֶחִי
שִׁנֵּי רְשָׁעִים שִׁבַּרְתָּ׃
לַיהוָה הַיְשׁוּעָה עַל־עַמְּךָ בִרְכָתֶךָ סֶּלָה (Ps 3,8-9)

Arise, O LORD! Deliver me, O my God!
For thou dost smite all my enemies on the cheek,
thou dost break the teeth of the wicked.
Deliverance belongs to the LORD;
thy blessing be upon thy people! Selah (RSV)

Commentators are generally satisfied with this traditional rendering of v. 9a, although Ravasi considers the verse 'wearisome' and probably a later stereotyped liturgical insertion.[49] Dahood argues that in view of the chiastic structure of vv. 8-9, previously identified by N.W. Lund,[50] where הוֹשִׁיעֵנִי אֱלֹהַי, 'Deliver me, O my God!' (v. 8) is balanced by לַיהוָה הַיְשׁוּעָה (v. 9), the *lamed* should be explained as vocative, 'O Yahweh, salvation!'[51] He adds that

> The prayer expressed in the nominal clause in the second colon of vs. 9, "Upon your people your blessing!", also supports the interpretation of [לַיהוָה הַיְשׁוּעָה] as a desire rather than as an assertion, "Deliverance belongs to the Lord".

---

[49] Ravasi, *Salmi* I, 122.

[50] N.W. Lund, 'Chiasmus in the Psalms,' *American Journal of Semitic Languages and Literatures* 49 (1932-1933) 288.

[51] M. Dahood, 'Vocative *lamedh* in the Psalter,' *VT* 16 (1966) 301.

This is also the view of Pope who adds that

> the noun [יְשׁוּעָה], "salvation", is used some ninety times in connection with acts of God, yet the unique statement that it "belongs" to the Lord is passing strange.[52]

He would go further and revocalise הַיְשׁוּעָה as הוֹשִׁיעָה, 'save'.

On the other hand, Miller points out that interchange of persons is not infrequent in the Psalms.[53] His first example is Ps 7,7-9 which begins with the imperative and vocative, continues with the third person in v. 9a and returns to the second person in v. 9b. Nevertheless, the third person suggests an expression of wish and therefore fits the context of 3,9 better than the flat 'Deliverance belongs to Yahweh'. Miller also refers to Ps 13,6 in which the psalmist after previously addressing Yahweh speaks of him in the third person. This is the final colon of the psalm and therefore does not form a real parallel to 3,9 where the final colon preserves the second person address. It is the penultimate stich that is in question. Furthermore, it is not merely a matter of change of person, for the expression of wish in 3,9a also disappears on the usual translation, which is not the case with the examples brought forward by Miller.

עֵת לַעֲשׂוֹת לַיהוָה הֵפֵרוּ תּוֹרָתֶךָ (Ps 119,126)
It is time for the LORD to act,
for thy law has been broken. (RSV)

καιρὸς τοῦ ποιῆσαι τῷ κυρίῳ (LXX)

---

[52] Pope, 'Vestiges of Vocative *lamedh*', *UF* 20 (1988) 205-206. Nevertheless, in Prov 21,31 is found וְלַיהוָה הַתְּשׁוּעָה, 'but the victory belongs to Yahweh', see Miller, 'Vocative Lamed', *UF* 11 (1979) 624.

[53] Miller, 'Vocative Lamed', *UF* 11 (1979) 623-624.

time for the Lord to act.

tempus est ut facias, Domine. (Vulgate)
It is time to act, O Lord.

Miller argues that the most natural translation of the syntax is, 'It is time to act for Yahweh,' but 'such a translation makes poor sense in the context of the prayer'. The rendering of RSV would reflect the syntax better if the phrase ליהוה preceded the infinitive; thus Hag 1,4 הַעֵת לָכֶם אַתֶּם לָשֶׁבֶת, 'Is it a time for you yourselves to dwell (in your paneled houses)?' Miller adds that since Hebrew word order in poetry is very flexible, the translation of RSV (and others) cannot be ruled out. He continues, 'The word order would allow if not encourage one to understand ליהוה as meaning "O Yahweh"'.[54]

There is also support from the Vulgate for this translation.[55] Pope shows that a number of later translations have leaned in this direction. He further observes that in this psalm the deity is addressed directly in the second person in 172 of 176 verses and that the ineffable Tetragrammaton יהוה is employed 19 times clearly in the sense of 'O Yhwh'. Miller and Pope draw different conclusions from this evidence. Miller in view of the late date of the poem and because other examples are apparently lacking concludes 'that the best one can do in this instance is place a question mark by the form'. Pope states that 'If Psalm 119:126a cannot qualify as vocative use of *l*-, it is hard to imagine what kind of construction could be judged convincing'.[56] Two possible cases of the vocative *lamed* have been proposed for Ben Sira:[57]

---

[54] Miller, 'Vocative Lamed', *UF* 11 (1979) 635.

[55] Consult Miller, 'Vocative Lamed', *UF* 11 (1979) 635 and especially Pope, 'Vestiges of Vocative *lamedh*', *UF* 20 (1988) 202.

[56] Pope, 'Vestiges of Vocative *lamedh*', *UF* 20 (1988) 203.

[57] T. Penar, *Northwest Semitic Philology and the Hebrew Fragments of Ben Sira* (BibOr 28; Biblical Institute Press: Rome 1975) 68.

הוי למות מה מר זכרך (Sir 41,1)[58]
Alas, O Death, how bitter is the mention of you.
האח למות כי טוב חקיך (Sir 41,2)
Aha, O Death, how sweet is your decree.[59]

The LXX translates simply Ὦ θάνατε, 'O death' both times, the Vulgate similarly 'O mors'. There is here no textual difficulty involving the proclitic *lamed* which in both verses functions in relation to a noun in the vocative.

While the translation of למות in Sir 41,1.2 is straightforward, the various renderings of Ps 119,126a illustrate the difficulty of interpreting Hebrew poetry. There is frequently more than one problem in a line. It is a matter of judging probabilities, and here the subjective element may loom large. Miller would accept the vocative *lamed* in this verse if it appeared 'with some frequency in Hebrew'. On the other hand, since there is so much that is obscure in the Psalms, one should not perhaps expect many 'clear' examples. It may be suggested that Pss 119,126a; 3,9a; Sir 41,1.2 provide sufficient evidence for a strong probability that *lamed* may function as an interjective 'O' whose effect is similar to that of a vocative particle. If so, vocative *lamed* may find its way into Biblical Hebrew grammar.

3. Vocative *mem*

Dahood suggested that Biblical Hebrew knew a proclitic morpheme מִי with vocative force. Since he only referred to this

---

[58] The reading חיים of manuscript B^{txt} is corrupt in the view of P.W. Skehan - A.A. Di Lella, *The Wisdom of Ben Sira*. A New Translation with Notes (AB 39; Doubleday: New York 1987) 467.

[59] Here חקיך is singular as in v. 3.

occasionally and incidentally while discussing other matters, many scholars are probably unaware of the proposal. It may therefore be appropriate to review the evidence that prompted Dahood to postulate vocative מִי.

Dahood maintained that vocative *m* can be discerned in Ugaritic. Thus he translates *ʾn mkṯr* (KTU 1.4(51).II:30), 'Look, O Kothar!', comparing *ʿn [gpn] wugr* (KTU 1.4(51).VII:53-54), 'Look, O Gapnu and Ugaru'.[60] The context is broken in both cases. Dahood argued further that this particle was employed in some Hebrew proper names. Thus the meaning of רַעַמְיָה (Neh 7,7) is generally admitted to be obscure,[61] as is that of the variant רְעֵלָיָה (Ezra 2,2).[62] Dahood would translate רַעַמְיָה, 'Shepherd, O Yah!', arguing that in Ezra 2,2 this name is reproduced as רְעֵלָיָה, with vocative -לָ- replacing vocative -מְ-.[63] Dahood also suggested the particle may be present in a few poetic passages.

מִקְצֵה הָאָרֶץ אֵלֶיךָ אֶקְרָא בַּעֲטֹף לִבִּי
בְּצוּר־יָרוּם מִמֶּנִּי תַנְחֵנִי (Ps 61,3)
From the end of the earth I call to thee,
when my heart is faint.
Lead thou me to the rock that is higher
than I. (RSV)

---

[60] = UT 51 II 30, VII 53-54, cf. M. Dahood, 'Ebla, Ugarit and the Old Testament', *Congress Volume Göttingen 1977* (VTS 29; Brill: Leiden 1978) 91 n.37. A. van Selms explains *mkṯr* as the passive participle of the D-stem of *kṯr*, 'brought into bondage', hence 'bondman', to be vocalised *mukaṯṯar*. He adds that 'It is evident that *mkṯr* is a servant (*ǵlm*) of the great goddess' [sc. *Aṯirat*], cf. A. van Selms, 'The Root *k-ṯ-r* and its Derivatives in Ugaritic Literature', *UF* 11 (1979) 742-743. See too *MLC*, 196.

[61] Cf. *HALAT*, 1183a.

[62] Cf. *HALAT*, 1181b.

[63] M. Dahood, 'Ebla, Ugarit and the Old Testament', VTS 29 (1978) 91.

Upon the lofty mountain, O Destiny,
give me rest. (Dahood)[64]

(60,3-4) ἐν πέτρᾳ ὕψωσάς με,
ὡδήγησάς με (LXX)
You set me high up on a rock, you led me.

cum fortis elevabitur adversum me tu eris ductor
meus. (Iuxta Hebraeos)
When the strong one is raised up against me, you
will be my leader.

V. 3 has been much discussed. The LXX apparently reads בְּצוּר תְּרוֹמְמֵנִי and תַּנְחֵנִי (from נוח 'to rest'). The Vulgate translates the same way, but Iuxta Hebraeos renders מִמֶּנִּי 'against me', while צור (without the preposition) is understood as the participle צָר. This is intelligible, but the preposition is not elsewhere used in this way according to the lexica. The difficulty with the MT is that it does not make good sense in the context. Gunkel points out that one would rather expect 'too high for my enemies,' and he follows the LXX.[65] Commentators who keep the MT do so without real conviction.[66]

Dahood sees in consonantal ממני the divine name מָנִי preceded by the vocative particle, here spelled defectively. The name could be explained grammatically as follows. The *yod* in מָנִי may indicate the hypocristic name. The root would be מני 'to allot' with the participial

[64] M. Dahood, 'Ebla, Ugarit, and the Bible,' *The Archives of Ebla*. An Empire Inscribed in Clay (G. Pettinato) (Doubleday: Garden City 1981) 299; id., 'Stichometry and Destiny in Psalm 23,4,' *Bib* 60 (1979) 419.

[65] H. Gunkel, *Die Psalmen* (HAT II/2; Vandenhoeck & Ruprecht: Göttingen ^{4}1926) 261. See too B. Duhm, *Die Psalmen* (KHKAT 14; Mohr: Tübingen ^{2}1922) 239: the request to be led onto a cliff that is too high makes no sense.

[66] Cf. Kraus, *Psalmen* II, 591 n.c; M.E. Tate, *Psalms 51-100* (WBC 20; Word Books: Dallas 1990) 110.

form מֹנֵי plus *-ay*. Dahood then vocalises תַּנְחֵנִי with the LXX. מְמָנִי would be parallel to the vocative אֱלֹהִים, 'O God' in v. 2 and form an inclusion with it. It is true that the suggestion requires a change in the MT, one that affects the meaning of the verb. On the other hand, the consonants remain intact and the proposal makes good sense provided that one is ready to accept the title 'Destiny' applied to the God of Israel.

The divinity מני could be found in Isa 65,11:[67]

וְאַתֶּם עֹזְבֵי יְהוָה הַשְּׁכֵחִים אֶת־הַר קָדְשִׁי
הַעֹרְכִים לַגַּד שֻׁלְחָן וְהַמְמַלְאִים לַמְנִי מִמְסָךְ
But you who forsake the LORD,
who forget my holy mountain,
who set a table for Fortune
and fill cups of mixed wine for Destiny. (RSV)

Here the reference is clearly to a heathen god. Dahood also finds the title in Ps 61,8 where the מַן of the MT has been variously interpreted

יֵשֵׁב עוֹלָם לִפְנֵי אֱלֹהִים
חֶסֶד וֶאֱמֶת מַן יִנְצְרֻהוּ
May he be enthroned for ever before God;
bid steadfast love and faithfulness watch over
him! (RSV)

διαμενεῖ εἰς τὸν αἰῶνα ἐνώπιον τοῦ θεοῦ·
ἔλεος καὶ ἀλήθειαν αὐτοῦ τίς ἐκζητήσει (LXX)
He shall endure for ever before God;
which of them will seek out his mercy and
truth?

[67] Cf. M. Baldacci, 'Due antecedenti storici in Is. 65,11,' *BeO* 20 (1978) 189-191.

The LXX apparently understands מַן to represent the Aramaic interrogative pronoun. The Vulgate does likewise. Better sense is yielded by parsing מַן with the RSV as the piel apocopated imperative of מנה with the meaning, 'allot'.[68] The imperfect יִנְצְרֻהוּ now depends on the imperative מַן, and the construction would be an example of an attested asyndeton.[69] There remains the incongruity of person between the two cola, which impedes the flow of the verse. To explain the MT recourse needs to be made to two very rare phenomena as well as to an abrupt change of person. It is not surprising that some reject the MT.[70] Dahood suggests reading מָנִ for מַן:

> חֶסֶד וֶאֱמֶת מָנִ יִנְצְרֻהוּ
> May the kindness and fidelity of Destiny safeguard him.

In this way the verse runs smoothly and, as in v. 3, אֱלֹהִים is balanced by מָנִי. The emendation would seem to form an attractive alternative to the MT. If Dahood's proposal for v. 8 is favourably considered, then his argument for the presence in v. 3 of the divine title מָנִי and of the vocative particle מִי becomes stronger.[71]

Dahood does not seem to have published any more examples, but he did propose some orally, and it may be worthwhile to consider them.

The first example is taken from Jer 10,17

---

[68] Cf. *GKC*, #75cc.

[69] Cf. Joüon - Muraoka, *Grammar*, #116i.

[70] Cf. Kraus, *Psalmen* II, 591 n.i, who deletes מַן. See too A.B. Ehrlich, *Die Psalmen*. Neu übersetzt und erklärt (Berlin 1905) 140, who revocalises to מִן on the grounds that חֶסֶד וֶאֱמֶת cannot be referred to the Lord.

[71] Dahood also proposes finding this divine title in Pss 65,4 and 74,22, cf. id. 'Ebla, Ugarit, and the Bible', in Pettinato, *Archives*, 299.

אִסְפִּי מֵאֶרֶץ כִּנְעָתֵךְ
יֹשֶׁבֶת[72] בַּמָּצוֹר

Gather up your bundle from the ground,
O you who dwell under siege! (RSV)

v.17a Gather O land your humility. (Dahood)

כִּנְעָתֵךְ is a hapaxlegomenon. The translation 'bundle' assumes a link with the Arabic root *knᶜ* II 'to draw together'.[73] Nevertheless, in Hebrew a root כנע with the sense 'to be subdued' or 'to humble oneself' is well attested and may be found here in nominal form. Since it is an abstract noun it perhaps follows the *qatalat* pattern and so can be vocalised *כְּנָעָתֵךְ.[74] Dahood suggests that the *mem* before אֶרֶץ functions as the vocative particle, 'Gather O land your humility'.[75]

The second example is provided by Mic 1,11

עִבְרִי לָכֶם יוֹשֶׁבֶת שָׁפִיר עֶרְיָה־בֹשֶׁת לֹא יָצְאָה יוֹשֶׁבֶת צַאֲנָן
מִסְפַּד בֵּית הָאֵצֶל יִקַּח מִכֶּם עֶמְדָּתוֹ

Pass on your way, inhabitants of Shaphir, in
nakedness and shame;
the inhabitants of Za'anan do not come forth;
the wailing of Beth-e'zel shall take away from
you its standing place. (RSV)

In the first stich, לָכֶם is plural and yet the verb it qualifies is singular. Some would therefore emend to לָךְ and even restore a 'missing'

---

[72] Ketib ישבתי.
[73] Cf. *HALAT*, 461b-462a.
[74] Cf. *BL*, 463 t"; Joüon - Muraoka, *Grammar*, #88Da.
[75] The term אֶרֶץ appears in the vocative elsewhere in Jeremiah, cf. Jer 22,29.

stich.[76] Wolff contents himself with reading a plural verb עִבְרוּ. He argues that the incongruence of gender between the feminine singular יוֹשֶׁבֶת and the masculine plural לָכֶם is prepared in v. 10a.b by the proximity of the feminine city names and the plural of their inhabitants.[77] Dahood tried to retain the consonantal text. Earlier he himself parsed the *mem* on לָכֶם as enclitic,[78] but then suggested making it the prefix of יוֹשֶׁבֶת with vocative force, 'O inhabitants of Shapir'.[79] This syntactic structure of imperative plus vocative *mem* exactly parallels the Ugaritic example mentioned above, *ʿn mkt̠r* (KTU 1.4(51).II:30), 'Look, O Kothar!'

In Cant 3,10, Dahood emended תּוֹכוֹ רָצוּף אַהֲבָה to תּוֹכוֹ רָצוֹ פְּאַהֲבָה, 'Within it there is pleasure and love'.[80] He takes the last words of 3,10 מִבְּנוֹת יְרוּשָׁלָם with the following verse, parsing the initial *mem* as the vocative particle and rendering, 'O daughters of Jerusalem', which would form a parallel with בְּנוֹת צִיּוֹן and yield a chiasm. The other six instances of 'daughters of Jerusalem' in the Song are also vocative.[81] Dahood's hypothesis on the presence of the vocative *mem* depends in some measure on his understanding of the preceding phrase, but granted the validity of the analysis, his proposal seems plausible within the wider context.

Our study of the clicits כ, ל and מ suggests, we submit, that in a few cases improved meaning results from their being interpreted as

---

[76] See D.R. Hillers, *A Commentary on the Book of the Prophet Micah* (Hermeneia; Fortress: Philadelphia 1984) 26 n.e; *BHS*.

[77] H.W. Wolff, *Dodekapropheton 4: Micha* (BKAT 14/4; Neukirchener Verlag: Neukirchen-Vluyn 1982) 12.

[78] Dahood, *Psalms* I, 147.

[79] The RSV's translation of cola 4 and 5 is the commonly accepted one, yet the third person appears incongruous amidst the second person addresses. Taking עֶרְיָה־בֹשֶׁת as a hendiadys one might render, 'Shameful nakedness has not gone away, inhabitants of Za'anan'.

[80] Cf. p. 85 above.

[81] Cf. Cant 1,5; 2,7; 3,5; 5,8.16; 8,4.

enjoying vocative force. In the case of ל and מ the presence of the particle in other Northwest Semitic languages supports this conclusion. The use of כ as a vocative particle on the other hand harmonises with its original function as a deictic particle. Its presence in other Northwest Semitic languages has not yet been demonstrated, but the possibility that they too witness to כ with a vocative function cannot be excluded.

7
Job 3 after the Discussion between Mitchell Dahood and James Barr

1. The Views of Dahood and Barr

The discussion between the protagonists took place in 1973 at the *Journées Bibliques de Louvain* which that year were devoted to a consideration of method in Old Testament studies. Dahood opens the discussion by quoting his own earlier remarks on the importance of Ugaritic for illuminating prepositions in the Hebrew Bible

> The Ugaritic use of prepositions and particles alone sheds more light on the meaning of the text of the Old Testament than do all the Qumrân Scrolls.[1]

He agrees with George Mendenhall that greater importance should be attached to texts which antedate the passage in question. Hence, the ancient Versions are judged to be less significant witnesses to the Hebrew text than are writings from the ancient Canaanite world. Dahood maintains that the evidence of Qumran and the Targums

---

[1] M. Dahood, 'Northwest Semitic Texts and Textual Criticism of the Hebrew Bible', *Questions disputées d'Ancien Testament*. Méthode et théologie (ed. C. Brekelmans) (BETL 33; Leuven University Press: Leuven 1974) 11-37:11. See too id., *Ugaritic-Hebrew Philology*. Marginal Notes on Recent Publications (BibOr 17; Pontifical Biblical Institute: Rome 1965) 26.

supports his opinion that the Aramaic translators of the first century B.C. found the Hebrew text as difficult as do scholars today. On the other hand these ancient authorities warn against emendation of the *textus receptus*.[2] A point emphasised by Dahood is that there are considerable differences within the Hebrew Bible itself, in particular between the standard prose of Biblical Hebrew deriving from the Jerusalem 'dialect' and Hebrew poetry from the north or from pre-monarchic times. At the same time the grammatical phenomena of Ugaritic and Phoenician will help the philologist 'to reduce the thirty percent unintelligibility of, say Hosea or Job, to more modest proportions'.[3] The implications of this are then spelled out. The traditional lexica and grammars will need to be updated to include Ugaritic and Phoenician material. This means that 'every single verse, above all the poetic texts, of the Hebrew Bible must be reëxamined in the light of Northwest Semitic grammatical, lexical, and stylistic data'.[4] Instead of judging the Northwest Semitic tongues to be distinct languages, he views them as dialects of a common Northwest Semitic language. Dahood states clearly that his method is one 'of virtually equating Ugaritic, Phoenician, and Hebrew'.[5]

James Barr comments on this new approach that 'the logically decisive step...often lies...in the fitness of the proposed interpretation for its context within the Hebrew biblical text'.[6] In other words it is not enough that the grammatical and stylistic phenomena of a particular verse be explained in the light of similar phenomena in other languages if the context of the verse does not support such an analysis. Barr observes that Dahood's method is not really

---

[2] BETL 33, 16.

[3] BETL 33, 19.

[4] BETL 33, 18.

[5] BETL 33, 19.

[6] J. Barr, 'Philology and exegesis. Some general remarks, with illustrations from Job 3', BETL 33, 39-61:42.

comparative 'but consists of *internal* elucidation within the unitary Ugaritic-Canaanite-Hebrew world'.[7] There is nonetheless a 'Need for each language to be seen and understood for itself'.[8] Barr considers that Dahood pays insufficient attention to the theoretical basis of his method, demonstrates 'an alienation from the sophisticated discussion of ideas, of entities such as theologies...' and ignores literary-critical solutions, for instance those of form or source criticism.[9] Dahood himself illustrates his method with an analysis of Job 3. It is therefore appropriate to see how he applies his method before considering the observations of James Barr. Dahood's own translation, stichometry and emendations will be given.[10]

2. Job 3,3-14

יֹאבַד יוֹם אִוָּלֶד בּוֹ וְהַלַּיְלָה אָמַר הָרֹה [הֹרָה] גָּבֶר (Job 3,3)
Perish the day I was born,
and the night that saw the conception of a man.

אִוָּלֶד Dahood notes the lack of the relative pronoun and the use of the imperfect אִוָּלֶד to express past action, phenomena common in 'Canaanite poetry'. With regard to the corresponding passage in Jer 20,14 אָרוּר הַיּוֹם אֲשֶׁר יֻלַּדְתִּי בּוֹ, 'Cursed the day on which I was born', he observes that the poet 'employs both the relative pronoun and the

[7] BETL 33, 42-43.

[8] BETL 33, 44.

[9] BETL 33, 58-59. A similar comment that Dahood's work lacks information on the literary context—style, genre, Gattung—and on the situational context—the social and political circumstances, the Zeitgeist—is made (during the same discussion of method) by J.F.A. Sawyer, 'The "original meaning of the text" and other legitimate subjects for semantic description', BETL 33, 63-70, esp. 66-67.

[10] The Hebrew text and its translation by Dahood are given in BETL 33, 19-22. Where he emends, the MT is placed in square brackets.

perfect form [יָלַדְתִּי] to express past time'. Hence, the Job text is not dependent on Jer 20,14.[11]

The use of the prefix conjugation to express the preterite has been the subject of some discussion, but it is widely admitted that in early Hebrew poetry, the form *yiktob* (from **yaktub*) can express the preterite.[12] At the same time, Waltke and O'Connor draw attention to the subjective element, for 'the Hebrew conjugations do not simply represent absolute time but the speaker's subjective representation of a state or an event'.[13] Job 3,3 is a case in point. The prefix conjugation is employed to express a wide variety of situations, and אִוָּלֶד can be interpreted as ingressive rather than preterite, 'I came to be born', forming a suitable parallel to the second stich which describes how the man came to be. At the same time it is clumsy to attempt to reproduce this nuance in translation. A simple preterite suffices.[14]

אָמַר Dahood claims that the verb אמר in the 'disputed' second stich signifies 'to see', rather than 'to say'.[15] It would appear that he is trying to circumvent the discussion about the meaning of the phrase 'the night said'. The ancient Versions interpret 'the night in which

[11] BETL 33, 22.

[12] Cf. M. Held, 'The *YQTL-QTL (QTL-YQTL)* Sequence of Identical Verbs in Biblical Hebrew and in Ugaritic', *Studies and Essays in Honor of Abraham A. Neuman* (ed. M. Ben-Horin) (Brill: Leiden 1962) 281-290; F.C. Fensham, 'The Use of the Suffix Conjugation and the Prefix Conjugation in a Few Old Hebrew Poems,' *JNSL* 6 (1978) 9-18; Joüon - Muraoka, *Grammar*, #113h; *WOC*, 496-501.

[13] *WOC*, #31.1.1g (p. 501).

[14] Cf. Driver - Gray, *Job* II, 16.

[15] Dahood postulated the existence of this verb in Hebrew under the influence of the Ugaritic verb *ʾmr*, 'to see' and 'to say'. Cf. M. Dahood, 'Hebrew *tamrûrîm* and *tîmārôt*', *Or* n.s. 46 (1977) 385-386; id., 'Abraham's Reply in Genesis 20,11', *Bib* 61 (1980) 90-91; Martinez, *Index* II, 64. Consult J. Sanmartín Ascaso, 'Semantisches über *ʾmr*/"sehen" und *ʾmr*/"sagen" im Ugaritischen', *UF* 5 (1973) 263-270.

one said'. The LXX for instance reads *καὶ ἡ νύξ, ἐν ᾗ εἶπαν* and the Vulgate *et nox in qua dictum est*, but it is unclear who that person is. As Pope observes, in poetry day and night may speak.[16] Habel keeps the MT and argues that it is the personified figures 'day' and 'night' (see Ps 19,3-5), rather than Job's parents, that represent his origins.[17] This offers a richer meaning than Dahood's 'the night that saw' and harmonises with the dynamic style of the chapter.

[הֹרָה] הֹרָה The Massoretic הֹרָה is generally parsed as qal passive[18] or pual.[19] Dahood revocalises to הָרֹה, the infinitive absolute, in view of הָרוֹ עָמָל, 'conceiving trouble' in Isa 59,4. While this does eliminate a hapaxlegomenon, the passive nonetheless discloses a grammatical parallel with אִוָּלֶד and fits the semantic balance between the two verbs.

גָּבֶר The sense of this word is 'man', but the LXX offers *'ἄρσεν*, 'male' and Jer 20,15 similarly זָכָר. Hence, some emend גֶּבֶר to זָכָר.[20] In support of the MT, Dahood points to John 16,21, 'in her joy that a man (*'ἄνθρωπος*) has been born into the world'.[21]

יִגְאָלֻהוּ חֹשֶׁךְ וְצַלְמָוֶת תִּשְׁכָּן־עָלָיו עֲנָנָה
יְבַעֲתֻהוּ כִּמְרִירֵי יוֹם (Job 3,5)
Darkness and gloom claim it,
a cloud settle upon it,
day's darkeners terrify it.

---

[16] M.H. Pope, *Job*. Introduction, Translation, and Notes (AB 15; Doubleday: Garden City [3]1973) 28.

[17] N. Habel, *Job*. A Commentary (OTL; SCM: London 1985) 107.

[18] Cf. *GKC*, #52e; *BL*, 286n'.

[19] *BDB*, 247b; *HALAT*, 245b; *DCH* 2, 592a.

[20] So *BHK*[3]. Habel, *Job*, 98 translates 'male' without comment. Others simply render 'boy' without comment, cf. Pope, *Job*, 26, 28; Clines, *Job*, 67, 69.

[21] See too Driver - Gray, *Job* I, 31; Clines, *Job*, 81, though he renders 'boy' (p. 67).

צַלְמָוֶת Dahood refrains from commenting on his translation. To judge from remarks elsewhere, he accepts the traditional vocalisation as a compound noun, though he attributes to מָוֶת the function of a superlative.[22] Barr observes that independent studies of the word favour 'shadow of death', the traditional understanding of the term, whereas the majority opinion in modern times favours 'darkness', vocalising צַלְמוּת, derived from a root II צלם.[23] Barr emphasises the importance of the older tradition for understanding the word. So he observes that 'out of the 18 or so cases in the Hebrew, about 10 or 11 are rendered with *σκιὰ θανάτου* in Greek', an argument particularly relevant if Job is a late book.[24] Barr points out that the history of the term is in fact complicated involving several different levels of explanation.[25] Barr does not reject the view that מָוֶת functions as a superlative, and his discussion of צַלְמָוֶת harmonises with that of Dahood. The difference lies in the nature of the discussion. Dahood never offers a full explanation of the term but accepts a view that he believes does justice to the immediate context and more generally to the literary context in Northwest Semitic. In similar fashion he has no difficulty with compound nouns in Hebrew and Ugaritic or with the superlative function of מָוֶת, but he does not himself attempt a

---

[22] Cf. M. Dahood, *Psalms* I, 147, citing D.W. Thomas, 'צַלְמָוֶת in the Old Testament', *JSS* 7 (1962) 191-200. On Dahood's view of compound nouns, cf. Dahood, *Psalms* I, 30 and id., *Psalms* II, 390 s.v. 'composite nouns'.

[23] In favour of the vocalisation צַלְמוּת derived from II צלם is H. Niehr, 'צַלְמָוֶת *ṣalmāwæt*', *TWAT* VI, 1056-1059. C. Cohen has argued strongly that biblical usage of the noun favours the meaning 'darkness'. He also asserts the relevance of the Akkadian evidence for a verb *ṣalāmu*, 'to be dark'. He would vocalise צַלְמוֹת. Cf. C. Cohen, 'The Meaning of צלמות "Darkness": A Study in Philological Method', *Texts, Temples, and Traditions*. A Tribute to Menahem Haran; (ed. M.V. Fox et al.) (Winona Lake: Eisenbrauns 1996) 287-309.

[24] BETL 33, 51-52. Dahood inclines to an early date, cf. M. Dahood, 'Hebrew-Ugaritic Lexicography XI,' *Bib* 54 (1973) 351-366, esp. 353.

[25] BETL 33, 55.

justification beyond noting similar instances in Ugaritic or Phoenician.

כְּמְרִירֵי יוֹם The expression is a hapaxlegomenon and the derivation of the governing noun uncertain. The ancient Versions offer different translations. The LXX reads *καταραθείη ἡ ἡμέρα* linking it with the opening of v. 6, 'may that day and night be accursed'. There is here no equivalent to כְּמְרִירֵי and it seems that the translators either ignored the word or had a different *Vorlage*.[26] The Vulgate renders *occupet eum caligo et involvatur amaritudine*, 'May darkness overwhelm it and may it be clothed in bitterness'. It can be seen that this Version ignores the word 'day'. Aquila reads *ὡς πικραμμοὶ ἡμέρας*, 'like the bitternesses of the day' and the Targum similarly מרירי יום.[27] It is not easy to see what this means. Later Jewish tradition connects it with demonic spirits.[28] This link is made in view of two passages in particular:

(1) Deut 32,24 where מְרִירִי is found in parallel with Resheph, usually understood as disease

> מְזֵי רָעָב וּלְחֻמֵי רֶשֶׁף וְקֶטֶב מְרִירִי
> וְשֶׁן־בְּהֵמוֹת אֲשַׁלַּח־בָּם
> עִם־חֲמַת זֹחֲלֵי עָפָר
> Wasting hunger, burning consumption, bitter pestilence.

---

[26] Consult L. Grabbe, *Comparative Philology and the Text of Job* (SBLDS 34; Scholars: Missoula 1977) 29-30.

[27] Cf. D.M. Stec, *The Text of the Targum of Job*. An Introduction and Critical Edition (AGJU 20; Brill: Leiden 1994) 20*.

[28] So Rashi and Ibn Ezra. This interpretation is basically accepted by Gordis, Grabbe and Michel. See the discussion in R. Gordis, *The Book of Job*. Commentary, New Translation and Special Studies (Moreshet 2; The Jewish Theological Seminary of America: New York 1978) 33; Grabbe, *Job*, 29-31; Michel, *Job*, 47-50.

The teeth of beasts I will send against them,
with venom of things crawling in the dust. (NRSV)

(2) Ps 91,6, where disease is personified as a demon

מִדֶּבֶר בָּאֹפֶל יַהֲלֹךְ מִקֶּטֶב יָשׁוּד צָהֳרָיִם
Or the pestilence that stalks in darkness,
or the destruction that wastes at noonday. (NRSV)

Nevertheless, it is questionable whether there is any reference to demons in either passage. In Deut 32,24 the parallelism rather implies that רֶשֶׁף is demythologised, while Ps 91,6 is most naturally understood as metaphorical. Grabbe and Habel point out that מְרִירֵי יוֹם anticipates אֹרְרֵי־יוֹם, 'those who curse day/sea' in 3,8 and that there may be a verbal wordplay between ארר, 'curse' and מרר, 'be bitter, hostile'. The 'bitter, hostile ones' would then be referring to demons of destruction.[30] All the same, most scholars have rejected the view that כִּמְרִירֵי יוֹם has anything to do with demons.[31]

Since 'bitternesses of the day' yields no obvious sense, another analysis of כִּמְרִירֵי becomes necessary. Syriac witnesses to a root *kmr* with the sense 'black, dark, sad'.[32] Although this root has not been found elsewhere in Hebrew, 'dark' fits the context, and scholars have generally accepted this derivation and revocalised to כַּמְרִירֵי.[33] The reference could be to eclipses of the sun.[34] Barr thinks that in Syriac 'be sad' is more central than 'be dark' and wonders whether the

---

[30] Cf. Grabbe, *Job*, 31; Habel, *Job*, 100.

[31] Consult for instance Pope, *Job*, 29; Clines, *Job*, 70.

[32] Cf. R. Köbert, *Vocabularium Syriacum* (Pontificium Institutum Biblicum: Roma 1956) 96b.

[33] Consult the list in L. Alonso Schökel - J.L. Sicre Diaz, *Job*. Comentario teológico y literario (Nueva Biblia Española; Cristiandad: Madrid 1983) 118.

[34] So Clines, *Job*, 68: 'eclipses' which fits the context.

movement from 'sad' to 'dark' may not be an isolated development of Syriac. He finds 'very little trace of *k-m-r* in a sense like "gloomy, dark" anywhere in Hebrew either before Job or after'.[34] Barr prefers the view that the derivation is from מרר, 'to be bitter', citing Sir 11,4 אל תקלס במרירי יום, 'jibe at no man's bitter day' (NAB) and referring to texts from Qumran. On the other hand, Clines points out that the sense 'be dark' is well attested in Syriac and that the passage from Ben Sira quoted by Barr has to do with a psychological state.[35] Clines observes further that the Hebrew verb קדר, 'to be black' takes on the connotation 'be sad' in Jer 8,21; 14,2. Dahood accepts the connection with כמר 'to be dark, swarthy' and believes the phrase is a poetic term for dark clouds. He goes on to compare the forms סַגְרִיר and *חַכְלִיל, also citing Ugaritic *amrr.k kbkb.l pnm*, 'Amrîr is like a star in front'.[36] The parallelism in Job 3,5 favours the view of those who derive consonantal כמרירי from *כמר, 'be dark, sad'. The reference may be to eclipses, but Dahood's rendering is consonant with the parallelism.

הַלַּיְלָה הַהוּא יִקָּחֵהוּ אֹפֶל אַל־יִחַדְּ[37] בִּימֵי שָׁנָה
בְּמִסְפַּר יְרָחִים אַל־יָבֹא (Job 3,6)
That night—gloom abduct it;
let it not be seen amid the days of year,
into the number of months let it not enter.

אַל־יִחַדְּ The sense of the Massoretic יִחַדְּ is unclear. If it is derived from the root חדה, 'to rejoice', the translation would be 'let it not

[34] BETL 33, 56. Barr finds support from Grabbe, *Job*, 29-31, esp. 31; O. Loretz, 'Ugaritisch-Hebräisch in Job 3,3-26: zum Disput zwischen M. Dahood und J. Barr', *UF* 8 (1976) 123-127:125. See too the discussion by Michel, *Job*, 47-50.

[35] Clines, *Job*, 70.

[36] UT 51.IV.17 = KTU 1.4.IV:17.

[37] Dahood revocalises יֵחַד.

rejoice amid the days of the year', on which Clines comments, 'but it is hard to see why being among the days of the year should be a particular matter for rejoicing by the night'.[39] Clines accepts the popular revocalisation to יֵחַד, parsed as niphal from the root יחד, 'to join'.[40] This undoubtedly yields fine parallelism and as Grabbe points out has good support in the ancient Versions.[41] On the other hand Grabbe argues that what seemed logical to the early translators and to us will have also appeared so to the Massoretes. If they recorded the word as 'rejoice' they will have followed a well-established reading tradition. He also notes the use of the verb שמח in Jer 20,15, where Jeremiah's father rejoices at the birth of his son. In the parallel passage in Job the day rather than the father rejoices. Dahood also revocalises יִחַד to יֵחַד but claims that יֵחַד 'is the Canaanite form of Jerusalemite *yēḥaz*'. In other words he believes that the verb derives from a root *חדה, 'to see', a dialectal variant of the standard verb חזה.[42] Dahood draws attention to a passage in the Ugaritic myth of *Aqht* where the goddess *ʿAnatu* offers the hero immortality and continues

> *aššprk.ʿm.bʿl*
> *šnt.ʿm.bn il.tspr.yrḫm* (KTU 1.17.VI:28-29)[43]
> I shall make you number years like Baal,
> like the sons of El you will number months.

---

[39] Clines, *Job*, 70.

[40] See G. Fohrer, *Das Buch Hiob* (KAT 16; Gütersloher Verlagshaus: Gütersloh 1963) 110; Pope, *Job*, 30; Alonso - Sicre, *Job*, 118.

[41] Grabbe, *Job*, 32-35.

[42] BETL 33, 24. Dahood does not attempt to justify this view here, but refers to proposals he has made elsewhere. The opinion is in fact highly controversial, cf. Grabbe, *Job*, 34.

[43] UT 2 Aqht VI:28-29.

Here too שָׁנָה and יְרָחִים are in parallel, a significant similarity in view of the rarity of the parallel.[44] Dahood concludes that 'This rare sequence, found in Job and Ugaritic, strengthens the identification of *yḥd* as Canaanite for *jḥz*'. At the same time, the biblical phrase בְּמִסְפַּר יְרָחִים, 'into the number of the months' resembles the Ugaritic *tspr yrḫm*, 'you will number the months'. There is indeed a striking literary parallel and it goes even further. In the Ugaritic text, the numbering of months takes place in the context of a desirable life. Even though rejoicing is not expressly mentioned, it is implied. This suggests that יִחַד, 'let it (not) rejoice' in Job was correctly vocalised by the Massoretes. Dahood's conclusion that in Job יחד is dialectal for יחז is therefore not compelling. The Massoretes would appear to be heirs to an old tradition. Emendation is not desirable despite or even because of our ignorance of what precisely is meant. The MT may be retained.

> יִקְּבֻהוּ אֹרְרֵי־יוֹם הָעֲתִידִים עֹרֵר לִוְיָתָן (Job 3,8)
> Let the Sea-Cursers damn it,
> those ready to stir Leviathan.

אֹרְרֵי־יוֹם The natural translation of the MT is 'cursers of the day'. Nonetheless many have rejected this meaning because the verse clearly alludes to the myth of the primeval battle with Chaos-Leviathan. Gunkel suggested that יוֹם, 'day' should be revocalised יָם, 'sea' in view of its parallelism with לִוְיָתָן, observing that the sea-monster Leviathan appears in parallel with sea in Ps 74,13-14.[45]

---

[44] The reverse sequence is found in 1 Kings 6,37.38. See M. Dahood, 'Ugaritic-Hebrew Parallel Pairs', *RSP* I, no. 572 (p. 364).

[45] H. Gunkel, *Schöpfung und Chaos in Urzeit und Endzeit* (Vandenhoeck & Ruprecht: Göttingen 1895) 59. See too Pope, *Job*, 30; A. Cooper, 'Divine Names and Epithets in the Ugaritic Texts', *RSP* III, ch. 4:rr (pp. 380-381).

Dahood with many commentators follows Gunkel, although he keeps the MT on the grounds that יוֹם may be the Phoenician pronunciation of יָם, 'sea'.[46] Clines observes that those who curse the sea must be on the side of order, whereas those ready to stir Leviathan into activity promote disorder, so that the parallel is less smooth than at first sight appears.[47] Gisela Fuchs replies to this argument by showing that אֹרְרֵי־יָם does not contradict הָעֲתִידִים עֹרֵר לִוְיָתָן. The stirring of Leviathan does not signify stirring him up to activity but rather bringing him to the point of exposing himself, giving his adversaries the opportunity to kill him.[48]

Even so difficulties with Gunkel's proposal remain. Barr points out that it introduces an element that is extraneous to the rest of the chapter which treats of *day*.[49] Habel agrees that sea and Leviathan can be considered a standard word-pair and that the audience would infer the parallelism. He continues

> by retaining the MT we preserve the development of the *yōm* ("day") theme, the allusion back to *m*ᵉ*rīrē yōm* ("the demons of the day"), the *yōm//yām* wordplay which is evident from the implied parallelism, and the clever irony of the "day-cursers" casting their spell on the "night" of Job's conception.[50]

---

[46] BETL 33, 24.

[47] Clines, *Job*, 86.

[48] Gisela Fuchs, *Mythos und Hiobdichtung*. Aufnahme und Umdeutung altorientalischer Vorstellungen (Kohlhammer: Stuttgart 1993) 66-67; see too K. van Duin, 'Der Gegner Israels: Leviatan in Hiob 3:8', *Give Ear to My Words*. Psalms and Other Poetry in and around the Hebrew Bible. Essays in Honour of Professor N.A. van Uchelen (ed. Janet Dyk) (Societas Hebraica Amstelodamensis: Amsterdam 1996) 155.

[49] BETL 33, 57.

[50] Habel, *Job*, 101.

Wider literary considerations therefore suggest that the reading יוֹם, 'day' of the MT is sound.

יֶחְשְׁכוּ כּוֹכְבֵי נִשְׁפּוֹ יְקַו־לְאוֹר וָאַיִן
וְאַל־יִרְאֶה בְּעַפְעַפֵּי־שָׁחַר (Job 3,9)
Its twilight stars be darkened;
let it hope for light—but none,
let it not enjoy the pupils of the dawn.

עַפְעַפֵּי־שָׁחַר Dahood explains this phrase as a 'A poetic term for the two planets visible at dawn, Venus and Mercury'.[51] Nevertheless, the precise meaning to be attached to the Hebrew *עַפְעַף is disputed. The lexica favour 'eyelid' or 'eyelash', although *BDB* notes that the word usually almost signifies *eye* and is found in parallel with עַיִן six times.[52] *HALAT* in fact translates 'eyes' in 41,10 and Prov 6,25, but renders 'eyelashes' in Job 3,9, observing that there already exists a Hebrew word for 'pupil', namely אִשׁוֹן.[53] It is interesting that the LXX which normally translates the term with *βλέφαρον*, 'eyelid, eye', here employs *ἑωσφόρον*, 'the morning star'. The Vulgate on the other hand offers, (*ortum surgentis*) *aurorae*, literally, 'the rising of the breaking dawn'. Clines concludes his discussion of the term by indicating that the arguments for and against the translation 'eyeballs' are finely balanced.[54] He comes down on the side of 'eyelids': 'the eyelids of the morning', which refer to 'the light in the eastern sky

---

[51] BETL 33, 25. Dahood claims that Ugaritic *ʿpʿp* denotes 'pupil', but this has not been generally accepted by Ugaritologists. Cf. F.C. Fensham, 'Remarks on Keret 136(b) - 153,' *JNSL* 13 (1987) 49-57, esp. 54. Inclined to accept Dahood's view is Pope, *Job*, 30-31.

[52] *BDB*, 733b.

[53] *HALAT*, 815b.

[54] Clines, *Job*, 71.

that heralds sunrise'.[55] Habel renders in similar fashion 'eyelids of the dawn', commenting that the phrase 'may conceal a mythological allusion to Shachar (Isa. 14:12)', the morning star.[56] Dahood's rendering is less subtle than 'eyelids', but 'pupils of the dawn' balances well the 'twilight stars' of the first stich.[57]

> כִּי לֹא סָגַר דַּלְתֵי בִטְנִי
> וַיַּסְתֵּר [וַיַּסְתֵּר] עָמָל מֵעֵינָי (Job 3,10)
> because it did not shut the doors of her[58] womb,
> nor avert trouble from my eyes.

וַיַּסְתֵּר [וַיַּסְתֵּר] The verb is traditionally drived from סתר, 'conceal', but Dahood proposes an infixed *-t-* form of סור, 'to turn aside'.[59] Now it is widely admitted that at least vestiges of the infixed *-t-* pattern can be found in Biblical Hebrew and it is *a priori* not impossible that the form should be found here.[60] If it is indeed so found, however, there is a danger of serious ambiguity which can impede effective communication.[61] In any case, the parallelism with 'shut' in the first stich seems rather to favour the traditional derivation of the verb from סתר, 'conceal'.[62] The allusive nature of poetry and of this chapter in particular permits words to connote more

[55] Clines, *Job*, 88. See Driver - Gray, *Job* I, 35.

[56] Habel, *Job*, 109.

[57] See too Pope, *Job*, 30-31.

[58] For a discussion of the suffix, see p. 75.

[59] BETL 33, 25.

[60] Cf. A.M.I. Boyle, *Infix-T Forms in Biblical Hebrew* (Diss. Boston 1969); *WOC*, #21.2.3b-d, #26.1.2; Joüon - Muraoka, *Grammar*, #53a n.1. Ugaritic does appear to witness to an infixed *-t-* pattern, cf. J. Huehnergard, *Ugaritic Vocabulary in Syllabic Transcription* (Scholars: Atlanta 1987) 320-321.

[61] Cf. J. Barr, *Comparative Philology and the Text of the Old Testament* (Clarendon: Oxford 1968) 175.

[62] See Clines, *Job*, 72.

than they would in prose, and it is possible that the ancient listener understood an allusion to the verb סור. If the audience understands more, that is its privilege, but the basic meaning remains 'conceal'.

> לָמָּה לֹּא מְרֶחַם [מֵרֶחֶם] אָמוּת
> מִבֶּטֶן יָצָאתִי וְאֶגְוָע (Job 3,11)
> Why did I not die enwombed,
> emerge from the belly and expire?
>
> διὰ τί γὰρ ἐν κοιλίᾳ οὐκ ἐτελεύτησα (LXX)
> For why did I not die in the belly?

מְרֻחַם [מֵרֶחֶם] Dahood's proposal is to read consonantal מרחם as a denominative pual participle from רחם, 'to conceive, enwomb', the reason for emending the text being the difficulty of explaining the preposition in Massoretic מֵרֶחֶם.[63] The apparent parallel in the MT between מֵרֶחֶם 'from the womb' (?) and מִבֶּטֶן, 'from the belly' falters owing to the ambiguous character of the first preposition. The second מִן is spatial but the first could be spatial or temporal. The LXX apparently takes the preposition to be locative, and the Vulgate with *in vulva* follows suit. Nevertheless, while the lexica recognise a locative function for מִן, with the sense 'off, on the side of', mainly with reference to the quarters of the heavens,[64] commentators are reluctant to accept this sense here. Temporal מִן usually bears the sense, 'continuously after,' but this is inappropriate in this verse. Driver and Gray propose 'immediately after' in view of Hos 6,2[65]

---

[63] Cf. M. Dahood, 'Denominative *riḥḥam*, "to conceive, enwomb",' *Bib* 44 (1963) 204-205, esp. 205.

[64] Cf. *BDB*, 578b.

[65] Driver - Gray, *Job*, II, 19; Clines, *Job*, 72. Cf. *BDB*, 581a (4a), b (4b).

יְחַיֵּנוּ מִיֹּמָיִם בַּיּוֹם הַשְּׁלִישִׁי יְקִמֵנוּ
He will revive us after two days,
on the third day he will raise us up.

It can be seen that the verse in Hosea includes two parallel temporal prepositions, which is not the case in Job. It seems doubtful that מִן can bear the connotation, 'immediately after' on its own. The alternative is to remain with the spatial meaning. A possible solution based on the elliptical character of Hebrew poetry may be mentioned. The suggestion is that the verb יָצָאתִי in the second stich may also qualify מֵרֶחֶם in the first, eliciting the translation, 'Why did I not not die (emerging) from the womb, emerge from the belly and then expire?'[66] On this view, the parallelism between the two spatial prepositions remains intact, and מִן is allowed its common meaning. Dahood's revocalisation turns out to be unnecessary in the light of Hebrew poetic practice. At the same time his rendering of the two finite *yqtl* verbs with a past tense is clearly appropriate.

[66] So L. Viganò *apud* Michel, *Job*, 61. On ellipsis in Hebrew poetry, cf. W.G.E. Watson, *Classical Hebrew Poetry*. A Guide to its Techniques (JSOTSS 26; JSOT Press: Sheffield [2]1986) 303-306. On verbal 'gapping' in particular, see M. O'Connor, *Hebrew Verse Structure* (Eisenbrauns: Winona Lake 1980) 401-404. It is true that ellipsis usually takes place in the second (or subsequent) stich, but this is not always the case. Translators often insert a finite verb in Jer 4,11aB, so W. Rudolph, *Jeremia* (HAT 1/12; Mohr: Tübingen [3]1968) 34 n.d; W. McKane, *A Critical and Exegetical Commentary on Jeremia*. Introduction and Commentary on Jeremiah I-XXV (T. & T. Clark: Edinburgh 1986) 95 (without explanation). It would appear that in the MT, יָבוֹא in v. 12 qualifies רוּחַ in v. 11. Consult R. Althann, *A Philological Analysis of Jeremiah 4-6 in the Light of Northwest Semitic* (BibOr 38; Biblical Institute Press: Rome 1983) 65-66 (= id., 'Jeremiah iv 11-12: Stichometry, Parallelism and Translation', *VT* 28 [1978] 385-391, esp. 387-388).

כִּי־עַתָּה שָׁכַבְתִּי וְאֶשְׁקוֹט יָשַׁנְתִּי אָז יָנוּחַ לִי (Job 3,13)
O that now I were lying
down and tranquilly asleep;
then would I be at rest.

כִּי־עַתָּה שָׁכַבְתִּי Dahood is unwilling to accept a causal or explanatory function of כִּי here and interprets the phrase as a precative expression, referring to other alleged examples of the use of כִּי as a precative particle.[67] This explanation of כִּי is controversial and not widely accepted. Muraoka has argued strongly in favour of a basically demonstrative function of Hebrew כִּי.[68] This would suggest the literal translation, 'thus now I should be lying down', which refers back to v. 11 and yields good sense. In idiomatic English it might be preferable to omit a direct translation of the word whose demonstrative force could still be reflected in the use of the present tense. Clines renders, 'Then I should have laid myself down in tranquillity', rendering עַתָּה by 'then', but this does not take adequate account of כִּי.[69] Habel offers, 'For now I would be lying in repose', though the strongly emotional context demands something stronger than an explanation.[70] Dahood's insight that the speaker is not merely drawing a conclusion but also forcefully drawing the hearer's attention to his desire for death remains valid even if there is no need to postulate an 'emphatic' כִּי.

---

[67] BETL 33, 26.

[68] T. Muraoka, *Emphatic Words and Structures in Biblical Hebrew* (Magnes: Jerusalem 1985) 158-164. See also W.T. Claassen, 'Speaker-Orientated Functions of *kî* in Biblical Hebrew,' *JNSL* 11 (1983) 29-46; A. Aejmelaeus, 'Function and Interpretation of כי in Biblical Hebrew,' *JBL* 105 (1986) 193-209.

[69] See Clines, *Job*, 68, 72. Clines follows Driver, see *BDB*, 774b g and Driver - Gray, *Job* I, 36.

[70] Habel, *Job*, 99.

וְאֶשְׁקוֹט / יָשַׁנְתִּי Though these words are in different stichs, Dahood interprets them as a hendiadys. This appears to be a *lapsus*. Clines and Habel show that it is the first two verbs that form the hendiadys.[71]

עִם־מְלָכִים וְיֹעֲצֵי אָרֶץ הַבֹּנִים חֳרָבוֹת לָמוֹ (Job 3,14)
just like kings and counsellors of the earth,
who rebuilt ruins for themselves.

עִם The preposition is usually rendered, 'with', even by those who accept the nuance 'like' in other passages.[72] Nevertheless, the context makes it clear that Job wishes to be with the dead kings not for their sake but because he wants to be dead like them. Hence, the comparative connotation is to be preferred.[73]

הַבֹּנִים חֳרָבוֹת The precise meaning given to הַבֹּנִים depends on the sense given to its object. Since Mesopotamian kings frequently boasted of rebuilding ruined cities, Dahood's translation 'rebuilt' is unexceptionable.[74] Habel translates 'built', 'assuming that the poet is using a literary device to describe the end result of royal building enterprises rather than the object of the building itself'.[75] The context certainly shows that this thought is present, but the next verse speaks of princes acquiring gold and silver without any such nuance being expressed. It is more natural to take v. 14 in a positive sense, 'rebuilt ruins', even though the context clearly includes the thought of the end result.

---

[71] See Clines, *Job*, 68; Habel, *Job*, 99; Pope, *Job*, 27; Alonso - Sicre, *Job*, 116.

[72] Driver - Gray, *Job* I, 37; Clines, *Job*, 68, though he concedes that the preposition 'is perhaps to be understood as "like"' (p. 72).

[73] Cf. Fohrer, *Hiob*, 14: 'so gut wie'; Alonso - Sicre, *Job*, 116.

[74] Cf. Pope, *Job*, 31; Clines, *Job*, 72.

[75] Cf. Habel, *Job*, 102.

3. Job 3,16-25

אוֹ כְנֵפֶל טָמוּן לֹא אֶהְיֶה כְּעֹלְלִים לֹא־רָאוּ אוֹר (Job 3,16)
Or why wasn't I like a stillborn in the Crypt,
like foetuses that never saw the light?

נֵפֶל טָמוּן Dahood analyses this as a construct chain and identifies טָמוּן as a designation for the underworld.[76] One important reason for the proposal is that שָׁם in the next verse requires an antecedent which טָמוּן when interpreted as a noun can provide. טָמוּן derives from the root טמן, 'to hide' and is generally parsed as the qal passive participle, yielding, 'Or why was I not hidden like a stillborn child'. In 40,13 the context and in particular the parallelism with עָפָר show that טָמוּן designates the underworld.[77] In 3,16 the matter is not so clear. Driver points out that v. 17 clearly refers to vv. 14-15, so that שָׁם presumably indicates the place where the kings rest.[78] Driver views sympathetically a re-arrangement of the text, whereby v. 16 is placed after v. 11. This on the one hand gives v. 16 a suitable position after the interrogative clauses introduced by לָמָּה in v. 11.[79] On the other it permits v. 17 to follow vv. 14-15 directly and so provides some kind of antecedent for שָׁם. This re-arrangement loses its point if טָמוּן is allowed to signify the underworld as it does in

---

[76] BETL 33, 27. He also finds this nuance in 40,13.

[77] Cf. Clines, *Job*, 73. See too Driver - Gray, *Job* I, 350; Fohrer, *Hiob*, 520.

[78] Driver - Gray, *Job* II, 20.

[79] The lack of לָמָּה in v. 16 occasions difficulty for it must then be supplied from the distant v. 11. אוֹ clearly does not continue vv. 14-15, even though v. 15 also begins with אוֹ. Nonetheless, this is a greater difficulty for the reader than for the listener to whom the narrator is reciting the poem. It has been argued that v. 16 serves a special literary purpose, namely to divide vv. 13-15 and 17-19, evoking vv. 11-12 and resuming its theme. Cf. D.N. Freedman, 'The Structure of Job 3', *Bib* 49 (1968) 503-508, esp. 504-505.

40,13. V.16 would then be the first verse in the chapter with a direct mention of Sheol. The grammatical argument alone is not decisive in view of the allusive nature of poetry, but taken together with the occurrence of טָמוֹן as a term for the underworld elsewhere in Job, Dahood's proposal becomes distinctly plausible.[80]

עֹלְלִים Dahood's rendering, 'foetuses' contrasts with the usual translation 'infants'. His rendering is apparently motivated by the qualification 'that never saw the light' as well as by the parallel with נֵפֶל. Since the emphasis is on death, 'infants' may not seem altogether appropriate, even with the qualification, but the translation 'foetuses' hardly imposes itself.

שָׁם רְשָׁעִים חָדְלוּ רֹגֶז וְשָׁם יָנוּחוּ יְגִיעֵי כֹחַ (Job 3,17)
There the wicked cease agitation,
and there rest those wearied by wealth.

יְגִיעֵי כֹחַ This phrase is a hapaxlegomenon and as Dahood remarks must be explained by the context.[81] The normal understanding of the expression is that it denotes 'wearied by strength'. This apparent contradiction is resolved by the explanation that the words mean 'wearied by exercising strength'.[82] Translations sometimes offer a paraphrase. So Driver simply renders 'weary'.[83] Dahood observes that in a number of passages, רְשָׁעִים connotes 'rich',[84] while כֹחַ sometimes connotes 'wealth' in Job and elsewhere,[85] and both

---

[80] It has been objected that טָמוֹן lacks the article (see Alonso - Sicre, *Job*, 119), but in Hebrew poetry the article is regularly omitted.

[81] BETL 33, 28.

[82] Cf. Fohrer, *Hiob*, 108: Krafterschöpften; Clines, *Job*, 73: 'exhausted of strength.'

[83] Driver - Gray, *Job* I, 37. See too RSV; NAB.

[84] 24,6; 36,6; 36,17; Isa 53,9.

[85] 6,22; 36,19; Prov 5,10.

nuances are deemed to be present here. An advantage of Dahood's interpretation is that it offers a straightforward meaning which does not require explanation. Possessors of wealth feature in the context (vv. 14-15), and the רְשָׁעִים with their כֹּחַ can be associated with the rulers and their possessions mentioned there. On the other hand, כֹּחַ usually signifies 'strength' and it is a matter of judgment whether it be understood in this sense or with the nuance, 'wealth'.

יַחַד אֲסִירִים שַׁאֲנָנוּ לֹא שָׁמְעוּ קוֹל נֹגֵשׂ (Job 3,18)
The Community of prisoners is at ease,
hears not the slave-driver's voice.

יַחַד Dahood believes that *yḥd*, 'community' is found in Ugaritic, but this remains uncertain.[86] At Qumran on the other hand the nominal function of יחד is well established.[87] It is widely accepted that the noun is present in Deut 33,5 and 1 Chr 12,18.[88] In v. 19 the term שָׁם requires an antecedent which Dahood provides by parsing יַחַד as a noun 'community,' when normally it is understood as an adverb with the sense of 'together, altogether'. Clines finds Dahood's proposal unacceptable on the grounds that it was on earth, not in Sheol, that the people in question were prisoners.[89] Nonetheless, the motif of Sheol as a prison is found in some biblical texts, and those who were prisoners on earth now find themselves in a new place of confinement.[90] Dahood's argument that שָׁם in v. 19 needs an

[86] Cf. Gordon, *UT*, Glossary 410a no.1087 citing UT 1056(KTU 4.224):7 *pqr yḥd*, 'the overseer of the community'. The tablet is damaged and the context incomplete.

[87] See A. Steiner, 'Warum lebten die Essener asketisch?' *BZ* 15 (1971) 1-28, esp. 9; H.J. Fabry, 'יחד *jāḥad*,' *TWAT* III, 595-603, esp. 598.

[88] Cf. Fabry, 'יחד', *TWAT* III, 598.

[89] Clines, *Job*, 73.

[90] Consult N.J. Tromp, *Primitive Conceptions of Death and the Netherworld in the Old Testament* (BibOr 21; Pontifical Biblical Institute: Rome 1969) 154-156.

antecedent is not compelling, as he has himself provided one in v. 16 by understanding טָמוּן as a term for Sheol, so that it would be to this noun that שָׁם in v. 19 refers. The apparent rareness of יַחַד, 'community' in the Bible makes commentators reluctant to accept this noun here, but it yields good sense. As the prisoners were a 'community' on earth, so they are now one in Sheol.

קָטֹן וְגָדוֹל שָׁם הוּא
וְעֶבֶד חָפְשִׁי־מְ אֲדֹנָיו [חָפְשִׁי מֵאֲדֹנָיו] (Job 3,19)
Small and great are there,
namely, slave, freedman, his master.[91]

חָפְשִׁימְ אֲדֹנָיו The second stich in the MT runs, 'and the slave is free from his master'. Andersen points out that this 'is not altogether satisfactory since the trend of the entire passage is that all social distinctions disappear in Sheol, not that *the slave* becomes a freedman there'.[92] Another difficulty with the MT is the lack of parallelism. Throughout the chapter there is regular balance between stichs. Only here is it lacking. In view of this, Dahood and Blommerde offer the version given above in which the second stich further explains the first. The *waw* is explicative and the preposition before אֲדֹנָיו becomes the enclitic *mem* attached to the preceding word. At the same time a number of objections have been raised against this reading of the text.

Clines objects that חָפְשִׁי is well attested in biblical texts but that 'freedman' is nonbiblical.[93] While it is true that חָפְשִׁי does not designate a 'free' man in the modern sense, normal biblical usage

---

[91] With Blommerde, *Job*, 39.

[92] F.I. Andersen, *Job*. An Introduction and Commentary (Tyndale Old Testament Commentaries; Inter-Varsity: Leicester 1976) 108.

[93] Clines, *Job*, 74, 97.

shows that it refers to a 'freedman', a man freed from slavery.[94] Secondly, Clines asks why a freedman should interpose between the slave and his master. The parallelism between the stichs elicits the answer that the three social classes indicated in the second stich balance the more general categories, 'small and great' in the first. It is true that two elements are paralleled by three, but the poet was surely sufficiently free to be able to alter customary parallelism to this extent. In v. 26 the final clause is balanced by three negations. Andersen observes that the suffix on אֲדֹנָיו is singular whereas a plural is expected and that a *waw explicativum* is less easy to believe than one of coordination.[95] Hebrew grammar in fact recognises that a suffix may agree only with the closer noun, but this does not exclude a reference to the first.[96] In the first stich הוּא similarly refers to both preceding nouns which it resumes.[97] The *waw* opening the second stich may simply exemplify the well known phenomenon in Hebrew parallelism of the second stich beginning with *waw*. The proposal of Blommerde and Dahood requires re-arrangement of the consonants and posits an enclitic *mem*. At the same time it offers an interpretation that harmonises with the general tenor of the chapter and with the strict parallelism it displays.

> לָמָּה יִתֵּן [יִתֵּן] לְעָמֵל אוֹר   וְחַיִּים לְמָרֵי נָפֶשׁ (Job 3,20)
> Why is light given to the tormented,
> and life to the bitter of soul?

[יִתֵּן] יִתֵּן Dahood remarks that there is no immediate subject for יִתֵּן of the MT and rejects attempts to make God the subject. Hence, he

94 Cf. N. Lohfink, 'חָפְשִׁי *ḥŏpšî*', *TWAT* III, 123-128.

95 Andersen, *Job*, 108 n.1.

96 Cf. A.B. Davidson, *Hebrew Syntax* (T. & T. Clark: Edinburgh [3]1989) #116 Rem. 1.

97 Cf. Driver - Gray, *Job* II, 21.

revocalises to the qal passive form with which 'the Masoretes were unfamiliar'.[98] The lack of subject can be explained by the verb being employed impersonally in which case it approximates to the passive.[99] Clines explains the lack of subject as due to Job's emphasis on 'the sheer fact of the inescapability of life' rather than upon the one responsible.[100] Yet in v. 23 God is explicitly mentioned, as Dahood observes. It is possible that we have here a case of the poetic device of 'delayed identification', the name of the subject being left to some time after its actions are described.[101] This does not exclude explanations of the type advanced by Clines and others but offers a stylistic justification. Joüon remarks that the qal passive 'disappeared little by little from the linguistic consciousness of Hebrew'[102] and it is a priori possible that some examples of it went unrecognised by the Massoretes. Nevertheless, several examples of the imperfect qal passive of the verb נתן may be found.[103] There is therefore no compelling reason for changing the MT.

> הַמְחַכִּים לַמָּוֶת וְאֵינֶנּוּ
> וַיַּחְפְּרֻהוּם מַטְמוֹנִים [וַיַּחְפְּרֻהוּ מִמַּטְמוֹנִים] (Job 3,21)
> who yearn for Death that they be no more,
> and who dig crypts for themselves.

אֵינֶנּוּ The literal translation would be '(who long for death) and it is not,' which must be understood in the sense 'it is not (available) for them'. The ancient versions already offered interpretations along

---

[98] BETL 33, 29.

[99] Cf. Driver - Gray, *Job* II, 21; Joüon - Muraoka, *Grammar*, #155 b. The impersonal subject is not necessarily God.

[100] Clines, *Job*, 99.

[101] Cf. Watson, *Poetry*, 336.

[102] Joüon - Muraoka, *Grammar*, #58 d.

[103] Cf. *BDB*, 681b.

these lines. So the LXX rendered, *καὶ οὐ τυγχάνουσιν*, 'and obtain it not' and the Vulgate, *et non venit*, 'and it does not come'. Modern translators often follow the Vulgate but do not usually offer a note on their rendering of אֵינֶנּוּ.[104] So Habel translates, 'who long for death that does not come'.[105] Dahood believes that there is here a philological problem which can be solved by recourse to Ugaritic. Thus he analyses this word 'into *ʾnn* plus plural ending *-û*', remarking that 'Ugaritic witnesses both *in* and *inn*, with afformative *nun*'.[106] The form then appears to be derived from a verb meaning 'there is not' with the third person plural suffix of the perfect tense.[107] Dahood's translation makes good sense in the context, but his analysis is open to question. A verb אין or אנן, 'not to be' is unknown, so that the analysis is quite speculative.[108] The derivation of the Ugaritic particle *in/inn* is uncertain, but Segert believes it may have originated from an interrogative adverb.[109] It seems safest then to interpret the MT in the traditional way, understanding אֵינֶנּוּ if necessary as a poetic ellipsis for 'it is not for them'.

וַיַּחְפְּרֻהוּם מַטְמוֹנִים [וַיַּחְפְּרֻהוּ מִמַּטְמוֹנִים] The MT is normally understood in the sense, 'and search for it more than for hidden treasures', for the verb חפר, literally 'to dig' often has the applied sense, 'to search for'.[110] Dahood selects the literal meaning, which requires a re-division of consonants. The suffix becomes datival and

---

[104] Cf. Habel, *Job*, 102, 111; Driver - Gray, *Job* II, 21; Alonso - Sicre, *Job*, 119.

[105] Habel, *Job*, 99. So too Driver - Gray, *Job* I, 39; Alonso - Sicre, *Job*, 117; RSV; NAB; NEB.

[106] BETL 33, 29.

[107] Cf. M. Dahood, 'Hebrew-Ugaritic Lexicography I,' *Bib* 44 (1963) 289-303, esp. 293; Michel, *Job*, 72.

[108] Cf. Joüon - Muraoka, *Grammar*, #102 j; *GKC*, #100 o.

[109] Cf. S. Segert, *A Basic Grammar of the Ugaritic Language* (University of California Press: Berkeley 1984) 77 (#55.7).

[110] Cf. Driver - Gray, *Job* I, 38-39.

plural, הוּם– being parsed as the third person masculine plural pronoun. Dahood allows the Massoretic vocalisation to stand, even though one would expect הֻם–, 'in view of singular *hû*ʾ and Arab. *hum*'.[110] This suggestion requires more proof to be accepted. In particular, the existence in Hebrew of a third person plural suffix in – הום needs to be demonstrated.

The term מַטְמוֹנִים, literally 'hidden things' is generally translated 'treasures', but Dahood prefers to take the literal meaning and render 'crypts' with its overtone of 'tombs'. He observes that 'the Greek *kryptein* means just this'. This suggestion is consistent with the proposal to translate 'Crypt' in v. 16. Here too Dahood's proposal harmonises with the context. Nonetheless, it is dependent on his analysis of the verb. The traditional understanding of the verse is altered and with insufficient basis in the text.

הַשְּׂמֵחִים אֱלֵי־גִיל יָשִׂישׂוּ כִּי יִמְצְאוּ־קָבֶר (Job 3,22)
who rejoice at the arrival,
are happy when they reach the grave.

גִּיל The expression אֱלֵי־גִיל resembles אֶל־גִּיל in Hos 9,1. In both passages the precise meaning is obscure. Its literal sense would appear to be '(who rejoice) to the point of exultation'.[111] On this interpretation, the second stich comes as an anticlimax. Others consider that in view of the balance between the verbs, a parallel for קָבֶר is desirable. גִּיל is accordingly revocalised גַּל, 'heap of stones',

---

[110] BETL 33, 29.

[111] Cf. Driver - Gray, *Job* I, 39; Clines, *Job*, 68: 'they would rejoice exultingly'. גִּיל, 'circle' may here refer to the circle of dancers who work themselves up into a frenzy. Consult D. Barthélemy, *Critique textuelle de l'Ancien Testament III: Ezéchiel, Daniel et les 12 prophètes* (OBO 50/3; Fribourg: Editions Universitaires 1992) 559.

understood as 'burial-heap'.[112] Nevertheless, it refers elsewhere when used alone only to the ruins of cities or to the mounds built over those executed.[113] Pope renders, 'grave', in view of the Arabic *jāl*, 'the inner side of a grave'.[114] These difficulties lead Dahood to suggest another option for גִּיל which he connects with Ugaritic *gly*, 'to reach, arrive' and renders 'arrival'.[115] This proposal removes the anticlimax and yields good parallelism. Dahood finds the same root in Job 30,14 in view of the parallelism between the hapaxlegomenon הִתְגַּלְגָּלוּ and יֶאֱתָיו, 'they come'. In 3,22 at least the suggestion seems plausible, although further study is necessary to demonstrate beyond doubt the existence in Hebrew of the root גלה, 'to arrive'.

Dahood translates יִמְצְאוּ, 'they reach'. That the verb מצא sometimes bears the connotation 'to reach' is widely accepted.[116] Some translations recognise this nuance here. So the NAB renders, 'and are glad when they reach the grave', and the NEB 'and when they come to the grave they exult'.[117]

לְגֶבֶר אֲשֶׁר־דַּרְכּוֹ נִסְתָּרָה
וַיָּסֶךְ אֱלוֹהַּ בְּעֹדוֹ [בַּעֲדוֹ] (Job 3,23)
to the man whose way is devious,
but whom God shields while he lives?

---

[112] Cf. Fohrer, *Hiob*, 112; F. Horst, *Hiob*. 1. Teilband (BKAT XVI/1; Neukirchener Verlag: Neukirchen-Vluyn 1968) 38; Alonso - Sicre, *Job*, 119.

[113] Cf. Driver - Gray, *Job* II, 21; Fohrer, *Hiob*, 112.

[114] Pope, *Job*, 33 with reference to A. Guillaume, 'The Arabic Background of the Book of Job', *Promise and Fulfilment* (ed. F.F. Bruce) (T. & T. Clark: Edinburgh 1963) 106-127, esp. 110.

[115] BETL 33, 30.

[116] Cf. *HALAT*, 586; S. Wagner, 'מָצָא māṣā'', *TWAT* IV, 1043-1063, esp. 1044; A.R. Ceresko, 'The Function of *Antanaclasis* (*mṣ'* "to find" // *mṣ'* "to reach, overtake, grasp") in Hebrew Poetry, Especially in the Book of Qoheleth', *CBQ* 44 (1982) 551-569.

[117] See too Clines, *Job*, 68.

נִסְתָּרָה Fohrer translates דַּרְכּוֹ נִסְתָּרָה, 'dem sein Weg verborgen ist' and comments, 'Das heisst, der sich verirrt hat'.[118] Dahood remarks that Fohrer's interpretation would fit better if נִסְתָּרָה were parsed as an infixed *-t-* form of *sûr* as in v. 10.[119] Nevertheless, the parallelism between the verbs favours the meaning 'hidden' for נִסְתָּרָה. Furthermore, Dahood's rendering, 'devious' necessitates a reference to the רְשָׁעִים of v. 17. This is possible, but it seems much more likely that the reference is to the sufferers who are the subject from v. 20.[120] Job throughout the book insists strongly on his innocence and he includes himself explicitly among the sufferers in v. 24. נִסְתָּרָה is therefore better derived from סתר, 'to hide' with the sense that Job's way is hidden from him 'so that he cannot see in which direction to turn'.[121]

בעדו [בַּעֲדוֹ] As Dahood points out, the emendation which yields the translation 'shields while he lives' depends on his analysis of the first stich. While it is true that the phrase וַיָּסֶךְ בַּעֲדוֹ is a hapaxlegomenon and that וַיָּסֶךְ in Job 38,8 is problematic, a sense like 'hedge in' fits this context and can be linked with meanings required in other contexts.[122]

כִּי־לִפְנֵי [כִּי־לִפְנֵי] לַחְמִי אַנְחָתִי תָבֹא
וַיִּתְּכוּ כַמַּיִם שַׁאֲגֹתָי (Job 3,24)
When my bread is before me, sobbing comes upon me,
and my groans pour out like water.

[118] Fohrer, *Hiob*, 109, 112.
[119] BETL 33, 30.
[120] Cf. Michel, *Job*, 74.
[121] Cf. Driver - Gray, *Job* I, 39.
[122] Cf. Clines, *Job*, 101 for this verse. Consult *HALAT*, 712a, deriving the form from I סכך, 'absperren'.

כִּי־לְפָנַי [כִּי־לִפְנֵי] לַחְמִי The sense of the first stich is obscure. Driver points out that if לִפְנֵי bears its ordinary meaning, 'before', the translation would be, 'Before my bread (= 'before every meal'), my sighing comes', which he and other commentators assert yields a poor sense.[123] In view of the apparent parallelism with כַּמַּיִם, they understand לִפְנֵי in the sense of 'like, as, instead of', hence, Driver offers with reservations, 'For instead of(?) my bread my sighing cometh'. There are two other passages where לִפְנֵי is sometimes thought to bear this sense. One is 4,19 יְדַכְּאוּם לִפְנֵי־עָשׁ, 'and they crush them like a moth'. The other is 1 Sam 1,16 אַל־תִּתֵּן אֶת־אֲמָתְךָ לִפְנֵי בַּת־בְּלִיָּעַל, 'Do not treat your servant like a 'בַּת־בְּלִיָּעַל'.[124] Nevertheless, Driver translates Job 4,19, 'They are crushed before the moth', that is, more quickly than a moth.[125] He also judges 1 Sam 1,16 to be problematic and favours deleting לִפְנֵי.[126] In view of the uncertainty about the meaning of the first stich in Job 3,24, Dahood here suggests repointing לְפָנַי, 'before me', though the meaning now would be very like that of the unemended MT, which is generally rejected as giving poor sense.

In 1976 Dahood wrote a long review of the second volume of *HALAT* and devoted several lines to the entry II לחם, 'to eat'.[127] He observed that in Ugaritic the normal verb 'to eat' is *lḥm*,[128] and drew attention to the longstanding repointing of MT לַחְמְךָ in Obad 7 to

---

[123] Cf. Driver - Gray, *Job* II, 21; Fohrer, *Hiob*, 112; Clines, *Job*, 75.

[124] Cf. Clines, *Job*, 75, 113; Fohrer, *Hiob*, 112 (but 1 Sam 1,16 is judged to be corrupt).

[125] Driver - Gray, *Job* II, 26.

[126] S.R. Driver, *Notes on the Hebrew Text of the Books of Samuel* (Clarendon: Oxford 1890) 14.

[127] M. Dahood, 'Hebrew Lexicography: A Review of W. Baumgartner's *Lexikon*, Volume II', *Or* n.s. 45 (1976) 327-365, esp. 343.

[128] Cf. *UT* 427b, Glossary no.1366. See too no.158 (p. 357a) for ʾ*kl*, 'to eat, consume'.

לֹחֲמֶךָ, 'those who dine with you'. He therefore proposed keeping לִפְנֵי of the MT in Job 3,24 but repointing the noun לַחְמִי to yield a verb, לֹחֲמַי with the translation, 'Even in front of those dining with me sobbing comes upon me'.[129] This second proposal offers a clearer sense than the first suggestion.[130] Nevertheless, there remains the objection that an alteration to the MT is not really necessary. If לִפְנֵי can connote, 'instead of', then clearly no emendation is required. On the other hand II לחם, 'to eat' is well established in Biblical Hebrew poetic texts. The question then remains open.

אַנְחָתִי תָבֹא Dahood argues that the genitive suffix of אַנְחָתִי may have dative force, 'sobbing comes upon me'. This phenomenon is recognised in Hebrew grammar and since the verb בוא more often than not takes a complement, the suggestion is attractive.[131]

> כִּי פַחַד פָּחַדְתִּי וַיֶּאֱתָיֵנִי   וַאֲשֶׁר יָגֹרְתִּי יָבֹא לִי (Job 3,25)
> When fear I feared, it overtook me,
> and what I dreaded came upon me.

The syntax of the verse is not entirely clear. Driver considers the first stich to be virtually hypothetical though no hypothetical particle is used

> For I fear a fear and it cometh upon me,
> and that which I dread cometh unto me.[132]

Clines prefers to regard it as a narrative sequence

---

[129] The particle כִּי is taken as emphatic, but it is also possible to translate it simply 'for'.

[130] This reading is accepted by Michel, *Job*, 75 but not discussed (not known?) by other commentators.

[131] Cf. Joüon - Muraoka, *Grammar*, #129h.

[132] Driver - Gray, *Job* II, 22.

For what I most feared has befallen me,
all that I dreaded has come upon me.[134]

Yet there has been no mention in the narrative of a particular dread of the hero. Hence, Driver's view appears preferable. Dahood understands the first stich in a similar way, though he interprets כִּי as temporal. In particular, he draws attention to Hos 11,1 כִּי נַעַר יִשְׂרָאֵל וָאֹהֲבֵהוּ, 'When Israel was a slave, I loved him', which, he asserts, displays the same syntax.[135] The *waw* of וַיֶּאֱתָיֵנִי is then parsed as the *waw apodoseos* and the suffix of the verb described as datival.[136] Dahood notes the parallel between the suffix and the prepositional phrase in the second stich and lists passages to show that this type of parallelism characterises the style of the book. Dahood's explanation of the syntax is plausible.

Dahood set out to examine Job 3 in the light of Northwest Semitic grammatical, lexical and stylistic data. Not specifically mentioned is the wider literary context. In v. 3 the significance of הַלַּיְלָה אָמַר is missed because no account is taken of this context. At v. 6 Dahood draws attention to a Ugaritic text with striking similarities but overlooks the relevance of the context of the afterlife to the question of how to analyse יִחַד. In v. 8 too the wider context supports the MT against those including Dahood who claim that parallelism supports understanding יוֹם as 'sea'. On the other hand the proposal to emend the text in v. 19 takes full account of the

134 Clines, *Job*, 75. See Gordis, *Job*, 39.

135 BETL 33, 31. See too Michel, *Job*, 78.

136 The more traditional term is 'accusative', see Driver - Gray, *Job* II, 22. Better may be to employ the term 'datival accusative' to describe cases involving 'a pronominal direct object where a prepositional object (viz. a "dative") would be expected' with *WOC*, #10.2.1i (p. 168) and n.13. Consult M. Bogaert, 'Les suffixes verbaux non accusatifs dans le sémitique nord-occidental et particulièrement en hébreu', *Bib* 45 (1964) 220-247.

parallelism found in the whole chapter. The grammatical parallelism of passive - niphal in v. 3 is slighted by emendation, but in v. 9 his understanding of עַפְעַפֵּי־שָׁחַר as 'pupils of the dawn' is plausible because it heeds parallelism.

Attention to grammatical phenomena is shown at v. 3 where differences from Jer 20,14 are noted. The postulation of infixed *-t-* forms of סור in vv. 10 and 23 is not plausible. The proposal to understand טָמוּן in v. 16 as a designation of the underworld is attractive as it has support elsewhere in the book and solves a grammatical problem. The explanation of the syntax of v. 25 by reference to Hos 11,1 is illuminating.

Among the lexical proposals, interpreting the verb בנה in v. 14 as 'rebuild' is plausible. The suggestion that כֹּחַ in v. 17 may signify 'wealth' rather than 'strength' is a not implausible attempt to deal with a hapaxlegomenon. So too in v. 18 the word יַחַד may denote 'community' rather than 'together'. On the other hand the proposed emendation in v. 21 must be rejected in view of the applied meaning of חפר, literally to 'dig' but often 'to search for' in other texts. The suggestion that אֱלֵי־גִיל in v. 22 may be explained in the light of Ugaritic *gly*, 'to arrive' is an interesting proposal for dealing with a much discussed phrase. Interesting too is the revocalisation of לַחְמִי, 'my bread' to לֹחֲמַי, 'those dining with me' in v. 24.

It can be seen that Barr's strictures are not without foundation. Dahood's proposals do not always fit the context and the appeal to Ugaritic is not always enough to support a new meaning (see v. 3 אמר 'to see'), while Phoenician spelling is not relevant to the question of יוֹם in v. 8. Dahood's lack of attention to the theoretical basis of his method comes out in his reluctance to discuss a word at the level of ideas. So for instance he posits the sense 'see' for אמר in v. 3 because he wants to circumvent the discussion about the meaning of the phrase 'the night said'. Dahood's lack of attention to literary-critical solutions comes out in his avoiding references to form criticism or other literary approaches to the text. There is a tendency to concentrate overmuch on the immediate context without taking the wider context or less obvious factors into account (see vv. 3 and 6). At the same time Dahood is not insensitive to literary considerations such as parallelism, nor to the fitness of words in their context. Some of his grammatical proposals are certainly worth considering. It is necessary to sift the suggestions made for Job 3 with care.

8
Conclusions

We have studied five different types of grammatical phenomena for which Mitchell Dahood proposed new explanations. In addition we have considered a longer poetic passage in which Dahood claimed to find a number of grammatical phenomena not included in standard Hebrew grammars.

With regard to prepositions, the differences between Dahood and other scholars have centred as much on the important theoretical level as they have on the practical. Where Dahood claimed for instance that the preposition ב sometimes *means* 'from', others have denied this, arguing that while such a translation may be desirable in certain cases, the reason for this may lie rather in a difference of perspective. At the same time a few passages remain where modern scholarship cannot yet give a clear answer either because the text is corrupt or for some other reason.

Dahood claimed to find quite a large number of examples of masculine **taqtul* in the Hebrew bible. Most of these can be explained either in terms of rhetorical effect or according to the well known principle that a subject understood as collective may govern a feminine singular verb. A few instances of the phenomenon cannot be easily explained in these ways, but it is still not necessary to postulate **taqtul*. Known grammatical phenomena and a certain poetic license can provide a sufficient explanation.

The argument that Biblical Hebrew knew a particle פ, 'and' is at least plausible in a few passages. It should be noted that they are all poetic.

Dahood argued that a number of clitics function in ways not generally recognised by conventional Hebrew grammar. He offered numerous examples of the 'vocative *lamed*', but most are not compelling. Nonetheless, there are a few cases where *lamed* appears to function as an interjection 'O' whose effect is similar to that of a vocative particle. A similar comment may be made about his proposal for a 'vocative *kî*' and for a 'vocative *mî*'.

Perhaps the most controversial of all Dahood's proposals is that Biblical Hebrew knew a third person singular suffix in *-y*. Our own investigation of the stronger examples of this alleged morpheme has failed to demonstrate its existence.

An examination of Dahood's analysis of Job 3 has disclosed a certain reluctance to consider the wider context of a problematic passage. Where he does take a characteristic of the whole chapter into account, as in v.19, he can offer a plausible suggestion.

It is probably true to say that Dahood's insistence on the reliability of the consonantal text is appreciated more towards the close of the century than it would have been at the beginning or even in the third quarter when he did most of his writing. There are various reasons for this change of opinion in the community of scholars. Very few of the emendations proposed by scholars have won general acceptance. The scrolls found at Qumran frequently demonstrate the antiquity of the received text. There is also growing appreciation of the value of related Semitic languages for elucidating the text. Here Dahood by his copious use of Ugaritic to illuminate the biblical text has made a significant contribution. Even if few of his proposals stand the test of time and if due caution needs to be exercised in calling on the resources of another language, yet his emphasis on viewing the Hebrew text in a wider linguistic setting remains valid.

Dahood never accorded the vowels of the MT the respect he extended to the consonants on the grounds that the Massoretes failed to appreciate the niceties of archaic Hebrew poetry. Dahood himself made a valuable contribution to increasing awareness of Hebrew literary technique.[1] The fact that he himself did not always take full account of literary factors in his philological studies does not materially affect the importance of his literary insights.

The contribution of Mitchell Dahood to the clarification of the meaning of the biblical text lies especially in his attention to points of detail. Even where his suggestions must be rejected—and he himself frequently changed his opinion on a passage in the light of later evidence—he offers a stimulus to providing a more exact description of lexical and grammatical phenomena. While his virtual equation of Biblical Hebrew, Ugaritic and Phoenician as dialects of Northwest Semitic has not won acceptance, the principle that our understanding of Biblical Hebrew can benefit from studies in the related languages is widely recognised. He would say that more needs to be done in this regard. We may agree.

---

[1] See for example M. Dahood with T. Penar, 'The Grammar of the Psalter' in M. Dahood, *Psalms* III, 361-456. One may also refer to dissertations directed by him and published in the present series between 1968 and 1987.

Bibliography

Aartun, Kjell

1978a *Die Partikeln des Ugaritischen*, 2. Teil. *Präpositionen, Konjunktionen*. AOAT, Vol. 21 no. 2. Kevelaer: Butzon & Bercker.

1978b Textüberlieferung und vermeintliche Belege der Konjunktion *pV* im Alten Testament. *UF* 10:1-13.

Aejmelaeus, Anneli

1986 Function and Interpretation of כי in Biblical Hebrew. *JBL* 105:193-209.

Albrecht, Karl

1895 Das Geschlecht der hebräischen Hauptwörter. *ZAW* 15:313-325.

1896 Das Geschlecht der hebräischen Hauptwörter. *ZAW* 16:41-121.

Allen, Leslie C.

1983 *Psalms 101-150*. WBC, Vol. 21. Waco: Word Books.

1990 *Ezekiel 20-48*. WBC, Vol. 29. Dallas: Word Books.

Alonso Schökel, Luis

1987 *Manual de poética hebrea*. Madrid: Cristiandad.

1988 *A Manual of Hebrew Poetics*. Subsidia Biblica, Vol. 11. Roma: Pontificio Istituto Biblico.

Alonso Schökel, Luis, and Cecilia Carniti

1992-3 *Salmos*. 2 vols. Estella: Verbo Divino.

Alonso Schökel, Luis, and José Luis Sicre Diaz

1983 *Job: comentario teológico y literario*. Nueva Biblia Española. Madrid: Cristiandad.

Althann, Robert

1978 Jeremiah iv 11-12: Stichometry, Parallelism and Translation. *VT* 28:385-391.

1983 *A Philological Analysis of Jeremiah 4-6 in the Light of Northwest Semitic*. BibOr, Vol. 38. Rome: Biblical Institute Press.

Andersen, Francis I.

1966 Moabite Syntax. *Or* n.s. 35:81-120.

1976 *Job: An Introduction and Commentary*. Tyndale Old Testament Commentaries. Leicester: Inter-Varsity.

Andersen, Francis I., and David Noel Freedman

1980 *Hosea: Introduction, Translation, and Notes*. AB, Vol. 24. Garden City: Doubleday.

Baldacci, Massimo

1978 Due antecedenti storici in Is. 65,11. *Bibbia e Oriente* 20:189-191.

Bamberger, S.

1923 Die Bedeutung der Qeri Kethib, ein Beitrag zur Geschichte der Exegese. *Jahrbuch der Jüdisch-Literarischen Gesellschaft* 15:217-265.

Barr, James

1968 *Comparative Philology and the Text of the Old Testament*. Oxford: Clarendon.

1974 Philology and Exegesis: Some General Remarks, with Illustrations from Job 3. *In Questions disputées d'Ancient Testament: méthode et théologie*. C. Brekelmans ed. Pp. 39-61. BETL, Vol. 33. Leuven and Gembloux: Leuven University Press; J. Duculot.

1981 A New Look at *Kethibh-Qere*. *OTS* 21:19-37.

Barré, Michael L.

1986 The Formulaic Pair (ו)חסד טוב in the Psalter. *ZAW* 98:100-105.

Barthélemy, Dominique

1992 *Critique textuelle de l'Ancien Testament: Ezéchiel, Daniel et les 12 prophètes*. OBO, Vol. 50, no. 3. Fribourg: Editions Universitaires.

Barton, G. A.

1908 *A Critical and Exegetical Commentary on the Book of Ecclesiastes*. ICC. Edinburgh: T. & T. Clark.

Bauer, Hans

1914 Semitische Sprachprobleme. 4. Zum Verständnis des Status constructus und Verwandtes. *ZDMG* 68:596-599.

Bauer, Hans, and Pontus Leander

1965 *Historische Grammatik der hebräischen Sprache des Alten Testamentes*. Olms Paperbacks, Vol. 19. Hildesheim [Halle 1922]: Olms.

Bergsträsser, Gotthelf

1962 *Hebräische Grammatik*, II. Teil. *Verbum* . Mit Beiträgen von M. Lidzbarski. Hildesheim [Leipzig 1929]: Olms.

Berthier, A., and R. Charlier

1955 *Le Sanctuaire punique d'El-Hofra à Constantine*. Paris.

Beuken, W. A. M., and H. W. M. Van Grol

1981 Jeremiah 14,1-15,9: A Situation of Distress and Its Hermeneutics, Unity and Diversity of Form - Dramatic Development. *In Le livre de Jérémie: le prophète et son milieu, les oracles et leur transmission*. P. -M. Bogaert ed. Pp. 297-342. BETL, Vol. 54. Louvain: Peeters.

Blommerde, Antoon C. M.

1969 *Northwest Semitic Grammar and Job*. BibOr, Vol. 22. Rome: Pontifical Biblical Institute.

Boadt, Lawrence

1975 A Re-examination of the Third-yodh Suffix in Job. *UF* 7:59-72.

Bogaert, Maurice
1964 Les suffixes verbaux non accusatifs dans le sémitique nord-occidental et particulièrement en hébreu. *Bib* 45:220-247.

Boyle, A. M. L.
1969 *Infix-t Forms in Biblical Hebrew*. Ph. D. Diss. Boston University.

Brekelmans, C.
1969 Some Considerations on the Translation of the Psalms by M. Dahood: I the Preposition *b=from* in the Psalms According to M. Dahood. *UF* 1:5-14.

Brent, J. F.
1978 /1979 The Problem of the Placement of Ugaritic Among the Semitic Languages. *WTJ* 41:84-107.

Briggs, C. A., and E. G. Briggs
1907 *A Critical and Exegetical Commentary on the Book of Psalms*. 2 vols. ICC. Edinburgh: T. & T. Clark.

Bright, John
1965 *Jeremiah: Introduction, Translation, and Notes*. AB, Vol. 21. Garden City: Doubleday.

Briguel-Chatonnet, Françoise
1992 Hébreu du Nord et Phénicien: étude comparée de deux dialectes cananéens. *OLP* 23:89-126.

Brownlee, William H.
1986 *Ezekiel 1-19*. WBC, Vol. 28. Waco: Word Books.

Burney, Charles Fox
1970 *Notes on the Hebrew Text of the Books of Kings: With an Introduction and Appendix*. The Library of Biblical Studies. New York [Oxford 1903]: Ktav.

Burrows, Millar

1950 *The Dead Sea Scrolls of St. Mark's Monastery*. New Haven: ASOR.

Caquot, André, Maurice Sznycer, and Andrée Herdner, trans.

1974 *Textes ougaritiques*, Vol. 1: *Mythes et légendes: introduction, traduction, commentaire*. LAPO, Vol. 7. Paris: Cerf.

Caquot, André, and Jean-Michel de Tarragon, trans.

1989 Textes religieux et rituels: introduction, traduction, commentaire. *In Textes ougaritiques*, Vol. 2. Pp. 7-238. LAPO, Vol. 14. Paris: Cerf.

Carroll, Robert P.

1986 *Jeremiah: A Commentary*. OTL. London: SCM.

Ceresko, Anthony R.

1980 *Job 29-31 in the Light of Northwest Semitic*. BibOr, Vol. 36. Rome: Biblical Institute Press.

1982 The Function of *antanaclasis* (*mṣʾ* 'to Find' // *mṣʾ* 'to Reach, Overtake, Grasp') in Hebrew Poetry, Especially in the Book of Qoheleth. *CBQ* 44:551-569.

Chomsky, William

1970-1 The Ambiguity of the Prefixed Prepositions מ ,ל ,ב in the Bible. *JQR* 61:87-89.

Claassen, Walter T.

1983 Speaker-orientated Functions of *kî* in Biblical Hebrew. *JNSL* 11:29-46.

Clements, Ronald E.

1980 *Isaiah 1-39*. NCBC. London: Marshall, Morgan and Scott.

Clines, David J. A.

1989 *Job 1-20*. WBC, Vol. 17. Dallas: Word Books.

Cohen, Chaim

1996 The Meaning of צלמות 'Darkness': A Study in Philological Method. *In Texts, Temples, and Traditions.*

A Tribute to Menahem Haran. Michael V. Fox, et al, ed. Pp. 287-309. Winona Lake: Eisenbrauns.

Cooke, George Albert

1936 *A Critical and Exegetical Commentary on the Book of Ezekiel*. ICC. Edinburgh: T. & T. Clark.

Cooper, Alan

1981 Divine Names and Epithets in the Ugaritic Texts: With Introduction and Selected Comments by Marvin H. Pope. *In RSP*. S. Rummel ed., Vol. 3. Pp. 333-469. AnOr, Vol. 51. Roma: Pontificium Institutum Biblicum.

1988 The Absurdity of Amos 6.12a. *JBL* 107:725-727.

Craigie, Peter C.

1971 A Note on 'fixed Pairs' in Ugaritic and Hebrew Poetry. *JTS* 22:140-143.

1983 *Psalms 1-50*. WBC, Vol. 19. Waco: Word Books.

Crenshaw, James L.

1972 Wᵉdōrēk ʿal-bāmŏtê ʾāreṣ. *CBQ* 34:39-53.

Cross, Frank Moore

1961 The Development of the Jewish Scripts. *In The Bible and the Ancient Near East: Essays in Honor of William Foxwell Albright*. G. E. Wright ed. Pp. 133-202. Garden City: Doubleday.

Cross, Frank Moore, and David Noel Freedman

1951 The Pronominal Suffixes of the Third Person Singular in Phoenician. *JNES* 10:228-230.

Dahood, Mitchell

1957 Some Northwest-Semitic Words in Job. *Bib* 38:306-320.

1962 Northwest Semitic Philology and Job. *In Gruenthaner Memorial Volume: The Bible in Current Catholic Thought*. J. L. McKenzie ed. Pp. 55-74. Saint Mary's Theology Studies, Vol. 8. New York: Herder and Herder.

1963a Denominative *riḥḥam*, 'to Conceive, Enwomb' *Bib* 44:204-205.

1963b Hebrew-Ugaritic Lexicography I. *Bib* 44:289-303.

1963c *Proverbs and Northwest Semitic Philology*. Scripta Pontificii Instituti Biblici, Vol. 113. Roma: Pontificium Institutum Biblicum.

1963d Review of *Il Semitico di Nord-Ovest* by G. Garbini. *Or* 32:498-500.

1964 Hebrew-Ugaritic Lexicography II. *Bib* 45:393-412.

1965a *Psalms I 1-50: : Introduction, Translation, and Notes*. AB, Vol. 16. Garden City: Doubleday.

1965b *Ugaritic-Hebrew Philology: Marginal Notes on Recent Publications*. BibOr, Vol. 17. Rome: Pontifical Biblical Institute.

1966 Vocative *lamedh* in the Psalter. *VT* 16:299-311.

1969a Hebrew-Ugaritic Lexicography VII. *Bib* 50:337-356.

1969b Review of J. Barr, *Comparative Philology and the Text of the Old Testament*. *Bib* 50:70-79.

1970a Hebrew-Ugaritic Lexicography VIII. *Bib* 51:391-404.

1970b *Psalms III 101-150: Introduction, Translation, and Notes: With an Appendix "The Grammar of the Psalter"*. In collaboration with Tadeusz Penar. AB, Vol. 17A. Garden City: Doubleday.

1971 Hebrew-Ugaritic Lexicography IX. *Bib* 52:337-356.

1972a Hebrew-Ugaritic Lexicography X. *Bib* 53:386-403.

1972b A Note on Third Person Suffix *-y* in Hebrew. *UF* 4:163-164.

1972c The Integrity of Jeremiah 51,1. *Bib* 53:542.

1972d Ugaritic-Hebrew Parallel Pairs. *In RSP*. L. R. Fisher ed., Vol. 1. Pp. 71-382. AnOr, Vol. 49. Roma: Pontificium Institutum Biblicum.

1973a Hebrew-Ugaritic Lexicography XI. *Bib* 54:351-366.

1973b *Psalms II 51-100: Introduction, Translation, and Notes.* 2nd ed. AB, Vol. 17. Garden City: Doubleday.

1973c Ugaritic and Phoenician or Qumran and the Versions. *In Orient and Occident: Essays Presented to Cyrus H. Gordon on the Occasion of His Sixty-fifth Birthday*. Pp. 53-58. AOAT, Vol. 22. Kevelaer: Butzon & Bercker.

1973-4 Vocative *kî* and *wa* in Biblical Hebrew. *Mélanges de L'Université Saint-Joseph* 48:49-63. *In Mélanges offerts au R.P. Henri Fleisch, S.J.*

1974 Northwest Semitic Texts and Textual Criticism of the Hebrew Bible. *In Questions disputées d'Ancient Testament: méthode et théologie*. C. Brekelmans ed. Pp. 11-37. BETL, Vol. 33. Leuven and Gembloux: Leuven University Press; J. Duculot.

1976a The Conjunction *pa* in Hosea 7,1. *Bib* 57:247-248.

1976b Hebrew Lexicography: A Review of W. Baumgartner's *Lexikon*, Volume II. *Orientalia* n.s. 45:327-365.

1976c Review of P.-E. Dion, *La langue de Yaʿudi* (1974). *Or* n.s. 45:381-383.

1977a Hebrew *tamrûrîm* and *tîmārôt*. *Orientalia* n.s. 46:385-386.

1977b Phoenician-Hebrew Philology. Review of S. Segert, *A Grammar of Phoenician and Punic* (1976). *Or* n.s. 46:462-475.

1977c Review of A. Lemaire, *Inscriptions hébraïques*. Tome I: *Les ostraca.* (1977). *Or* n.s. 46:329-331.

1978a Ebla, Ugarit and the Old Testament. *In Congress Volume Göttingen 1977*. Pp. 81-112. VTS, Vol. 29. Leiden: Brill.

1978b New Readings in Lamentations. *Bib* 59:174-197.

1979a Stichometry and Destiny in Psalm 23,4. *Bib* 60:417-419.

1979b Third Masculine Singular with Preformative *t-* in Northwest Semitic. *Or* n.s. 48:97-106.

1980a Abraham's Reply in Genesis 20,11. *Bib* 61:90-91.

1980b Can One Plow Without Oxen? (Amos 6:12): A Study of *ba-* and *ʿal*. *In The Bible World: Essays in Honor of Cyrus H. Gordon*. G. Rendsburg ed. Pp. 13-23. New York: Ktav.

1981a Ebla, Ugarit, and the Bible. Afterword. *In The Archives of Ebla: An Empire Inscribed in Clay*. By Giovanni Pettinato. Pp. 271-321. Garden City: Doubleday.

1981b Ugaritic-Hebrew Parallel Pairs Supplement. *In RSP*. S. Rummel ed., Vol. 3. Pp. 178-206. AnOr, Vol. 51. Roma: Pontificium Institutum Biblicum.

1981c Ugaritic-Hebrew Parallel Pairs. *In RSP*. S. Rummel ed., Vol. 3. Pp. 1-178. AnOr, Vol. 51. Roma: Pontificium Institutum Biblicum.

1982 Review of K. Aartun, *Die Partikeln des Ugaritischen*, 2. Teil. *Präpositionen, Konjunktionen* (1978). *Or* n.s. 51:281-283.

1986 The Moabite Stone and Northwest Semitic Philology. *In The Archaeology of Jordan and Other Studies: Presented to Siegfried H. Horn*. L. T. Geraty and L. G. Herr ed. Pp. 429-441. Berrien Springs: Andrews University Press.

Davidson, Andrew Bruce

1989 *Hebrew Syntax*. 3rd ed. Edinburgh: T & T Clark.

Delitzsch, Friedrich

1889 *Commentar über das Buch Jesaia*. Leipzig.

Dietrich, Manfried, and Oswald Loretz

1980 Zweifelhafte Belege für *m(n)* 'von': zur ugaritischen Lexikographie (XVI). *UF* 12:183-187.

1986 Die bipolare Position von *ʿl* im Ugaritischen und Hebräischen. *UF* 18:449-450.

Dietrich, Manfried, Oswald Loretz, and Joachín Sanmartín
1995 *The Cuneiform Alphabetic Texts from Ugarit, Ras Ibn Hani and Other Places.* KTU Edition No. 2. Abhandlungen zur Literatur Alt-Syrien-Palästinas und Mesopotamiens, Vol. 8. Münster: Ugarit-Verlag.

Dijk, Hubert J. van
1969 Does Third Masculine Singular **taqtul* Exist in Hebrew? *VT* 19:440-447.

Dion, Paul-E.
1974 *La langue de Yaʿudi: description et classement de l'ancien parler de Zencirli dans le cadre des langues sémitiques du nord-ouest.* Studies in Religion. Ontario: The Corporation for the Publication of Academic Studies in Religion in Canada.

Dobrusin, Deborah L.
1981 The Third Masculine Plural of the Prefixed Form of the Verb in Ugaritic. *JANES* 13:5-14.

Donner, Herbert
1967 Ugaritismen in der Psalmenforschung. *ZAW* 79:322-350.

Doyle, Brian
1996 Psalm 58: Curse as Voiced Disorientation. *Bijdragen* 57:122-148.

Driver, Samuel R.
1890 *Notes on the Hebrew Text of the Books of Samuel.* Oxford: Clarendon.
1901 *A Critical and Exegetical Commentary on Deuteronomy.* 3rd ed. ICC. Edinburgh: T. & T. Clark.

Driver, Samuel R., and George B. Gray
1921 *A Critical and Exegetical Commentary on the Book of Job Together with a New Translation.* ICC. Edinburgh: T. & T. Clark.

Duhm, Bernhard

1914 *Das Buch Jesaia*. 3rd ed. Göttingen: Vandenhoeck & Ruprecht.

1922 *Die Psalmen*. 2nd ed. KHKAT, Vol. 14. Tübingen: Mohr.

Ehrlich, Arnold B.

1905 *Die Psalmen: neu übersetzt und erklärt*. Berlin.

1912 *Randglossen zur hebräischen Bibel: Textkritisches, Sprachliches und Sachliches*, Vol. 4. Leipzig: J.C. Hinrichs.

1914 *Randglossen zur hebräischen Bibel: Textkritisches, Sprachliches und Sachliches*, Vol. 7. Leipzig: J.C. Hinrichs.

1918 *Randglossen zur hebräischen Bibel: Textkritisches, Sprachliches und Sachliches*, Vol. 6. Leipzig: J.C. Hinrichs.

Elliger, Karl

1978 *Deuterojesaja, 1. Teilband. Jesaja 40,1-45,7*. BKAT, Vol. 11/1. Neukirchen-Vluyn: Neukirchener Verlag.

Emerton, John A.

1996 Are There Examples of Enclitic *Mem* in the Hebrew Bible? *In Texts, Temples, and Traditions: A Tribute to Menahem Haran*. Ed. Michael V. Fox et al. Pp. 321-338. Winona Lake: Eisenbrauns.

Fabry, Heinz-Josef

1980 יחד *jāḥad*. *In TWAT*, Vol. 3. Col. 595-603.

Fensham, Frank Charles

1987 Remarks on Keret 136(b) - 153. *JNSL* 13:49-57.

Fohrer, Georg

1963 *Das Buch Hiob*. KAT, Vol. 16. Gütersloher Verlagshaus: Gütersloh.

Fredericks, Daniel C.

1996 A North Israelite Dialect in the Hebrew Bible? Questions of Methodology. *Hebrew Studies* 37:7-20.

Freedman, David Noel

1968 The Structure of Job 3. *Bib* 49:503-508.

Friedrich, Johannes, and Wolfgang Röllig

1970 *Phönizisch-Punische Grammatik*. 2nd ed. AnOr, Vol. 46. Roma: Pontificium Institutum Biblicum.

Fuchs, Gisela

1993 *Mythos und Hiobdichtung: Aufnahme und Umdeutung altorientalischer Vorstellungen*. Stuttgart: Kohlhammer.

Fuentes Estañol, María-José

1980 *Vocabulario Fenicio*. Biblioteca Fenicia, Vol. 1. Barcelona: Consejo Superior de Investigaciones Científicas.

Futato, M. D.

1978-9 The Preposition 'beth' in the Hebrew Psalter. *WTJ* 41:68-83.

Garbini, Giovanni

1960 *Il semitico di nord-ovest*. Napoli: Istituto Universitario Orientale Di Napoli.

Gerleman, Gillis

1965 *Ruth: das Hohelied*. BKAT, Vol. 18. Neukirchen-Vluyn: Neukirchener Verlag.

Gevirtz, Stanley

1973 On Canaanite Rhetoric: The Evidence of the Amarna Letters from Tyre. *Orientalia* 42:162-177.

Gibson, John C. L.

1973 *Textbook of Syrian Semitic Inscriptions*, Vol. 1: *Hebrew and Moabite Inscriptions*. Oxford: Clarendon.

1978 *Canaanite Myths and Legends*. 2nd ed. Edinburgh: T. & T. Clark.

Ginsberg, H. L.

1936 The Rebellion and Death of Baʿlu. *Or* n.s. 5:161-198.

Globe, A.

1975 The Muster of the Tribes in Judges 5 11e-18. *ZAW* 87:169-184.

Gordis, Robert

1978 *The Book of Job: Commentary, New Translation and Special Studies*. Moreshet, Vol. 2. New York: The Jewish Theological Seminary of America.

Gordon, Cyrus H.

1955 North Israelite Influence on Postexilic Hebrew. *IEJ* 5:85-88.

1965 *Ugaritic Textbook*. AnOr, Vol. 38. Roma: Pontificium Institutum Biblicum.

1981 'In' of Predication or Equivalence. *JBL* 100:612-613.

Grabbe, Lester L.

1977 *Comparative Philology and the Text of Job*. SBLDS, Vol. 34. Missoula: Scholars.

Gray, George B.

1912 *A Critical and Exegetical Commentary on the Book of Isaiah I-XXVII*. ICC. Edinburgh: T. & T. Clark.

Gray, John

1977 A Cantata of the Autumn Festival: Psalm LXVIII. *JSS* 22:2-26.

Greenberg, Moshe

1983 *Ezekiel 1-20: A New Translation with Introduction and Commentary*. AB, Vol. 22. Garden City: Doubleday.

Grossberg, Daniel

1980 Noun Verb Parallelism: Syntactic or Asyntactic? *JBL* 99:481-488.

Guillaume, Alfred

1963 The Arabic Background of the Book of Job. *In Promise and Fulfilment*. F. F. Bruce ed. Pp. 106-127. Edinburgh: T. & T. Clark.

Gunkel, Hermann

1895 *Schöpfung und Chaos in Urzeit und Endzeit*. Göttingen: Vandenhoeck & Ruprecht.

1926 *Die Psalmen*. 4th ed. HAT, Vol. II/2. Göttingen: Vandenhoeck & Ruprecht.

Habel, Norman C.

1985 *The Book of Job: A Commentary*. OTL. Philadelphia: Westminster.

Harper, William R.

1904 *A Critical and Exegetical Commentary on Amos and Hosea*. ICC. Edinburgh: T. & T. Clark.

Healey, John F.

1984 The Immortality of the King: Ugarit and the Psalms. *Or* n.s. 53:245-254. *In Memorial Mitchell J. Dahood.*

Held, Moshe

1962 The *YQTL-QTL (QTL-YQTL)* Sequence of Identical Verbs in Biblical Hebrew and in Ugaritic. *In Studies and Essays in Honor of Abraham A. Neuman*. M. Ben-Horin ed. Pp. 281-290. Leiden: Brill.

Hertzberg, Hans Wilhelm

1963 *Der Prediger*. KAT, Vol. 17/4. Gütersloh: Mohn.

Hillers, Delbert R.

1984 *A Commentary on the Book of the Prophet Micah*. Hermeneia. Philadelphia: Fortress.

1992 *Lamentations: A New Translation with Introduction and Commentary*. 2nd ed. AB, Vol. 7A. New York: Doubleday.

Hoftijzer, Jean, and K. Jongeling

1995 *Dictionary of the North-West Semitic Inscriptions: Part I ʾ - L: Part II M - T*. Appendices by R. C. Steiner, A. Mosak Moshavi, and B. Porten. Handbook of Oriental

Studies I, The Near and Middle East, Vol. 21-22. Leiden: Brill.

Holladay, William L.

1986 *Jeremiah: A Commentary on the Book of the Prophet Jeremiah Chapters 1-25*. Hermeneia. Philadelphia: Fortress.

1989 *Jeremiah: A Commentary on the Book of the Prophet Jeremiah Chapters 26-52*. Hermeneia. Philadelphia: Fortress.

Hoonacker, A. van

1908 *Les douze petits prophètes*. Paris: Gabalda.

Horst, Friedrich

1968 *Hiob, 1. Teilband*. BKAT, Vol. XVI no. 1. Neukirchen-Vluyn: Neukirchener Verlag.

Hospers, Johannes H.

1988 Das Problem der sogenannten semantischen Polarität im Althebräischen. *ZAH* 1:32-39.

Huehnergard, John

1983 Asseverative **la* and Hypothetical **lu/law* in Semitic. *JAOS* 103:569-593.

1987 *Ugaritic Vocabulary in Syllabic Transcription*. Atlanta: Scholars.

Hummel, Horace D.

1957 Enclitic *mem* in Early Northwest Semitic, Especially Hebrew. *JBL* 76:85-107.

Irwin, William H.

1977 *Isaiah 28-33 Translation with Philological Notes*. BibOr, Vol. 30. Rome: Biblical Institute Press.

Jackson, Kent P.

1989 The Language of the Meshaʿ Inscription. *In Studies in the Mesha Inscription and Moab*. Andrew Dearman ed.

Pp. 96-130. Archaeology and Biblical Studies, Vol. 2. Atlanta: Scholars.

Janzen, J. Gerald

1973 *Studies in the Text of Jeremiah.* HSM, Vol. 6. Cambridge: Harvard University Press.

Jenni, Ernst

1968 *Das hebräische Piʿel: syntaktisch-semasiologische Untersuchung einer Verbalform im Alten Testament.* Zürich: EVZ.

1992 *Die hebräischen Präpositionen*, Vol. 1: *Die Präposition Beth*. Stuttgart: Kohlhammer.

Joüon, Paul

1909 *Le Cantique des Cantiques*. Paris: Beauchesne.

1991 *A Grammar of Biblical Hebrew.* Rev. and Trans. Takamitsu Muraoka. Subsidia Biblica, Vol. 14. Roma: Pontificio Istituto Biblico.

Kaiser, Otto

1973 *Der Prophet Jesaja: Kapitel 13-39*. ATD, Vol. 18. Göttingen: Vandenhoeck & Ruprecht.

Köbert, Raimund

1956 *Vocabularium Syriacum.* Roma: Pontificium Institutum Biblicum.

Krahmalkov, Charles R.

1970 Studies in Phoenician and Punic Grammar. *JSS* 15:181-188.

Kraus, Hans-Joachim

1956 *Klagelieder (Threni)*. BKAT, Vol. 20. Neukirchen-Vluyn: Neukirchener Verlag.

1978 *Psalmen*. 5th ed. BKAT, Vol. 15/1-2. Neukirchen-Vluyn: Neukirchener Verlag.

Kuhnigk, Willibald

1974 *Nordwestsemitische Studien zum Hoseabuch*. BibOr, Vol. 27. Rome: Biblical Institute Press.

Lauha, Aarre

1978 *Kohelet*. BKAT, Vol. 19. Neukirchen: Neukirchener Verlag.

Levi, Jaakov

1987 *Die Inkongruenz im biblischen Hebräisch*. Wiesbaden: Harrassowitz.

Lipiński, Edward

1981 Aḫat-Milki, reine d'Ugarit, et la guerre de Mukiš. *OLP* 12:79-115.

Loewenstamm, Samuel E.

1975 Ugarit and the Bible: I. *Bib* 76:103-119.

Lohfink, Norbert

1977 חָפְשִׁי *ḥŏpšî*. *In TWAT*, Vol. 3. Col. 123-128.

1982 יָרַשׁ *jāraš*. *In TWAT*, Vol. 3. Col. 953-985.

1983 Die Bedeutung von hebr. *jrš qal* und *hif*. *BZ* N.F. 27:14-33.

Loretz, Oswald

1976 Ugaritisch-Hebräisch in Job 3,3-26: zum Disput zwischen M. Dahood und J. Barr. *UF* 8:123-127.

1989a Amos vi 12. *VT* 39:240-242.

1989b Ugaritisch *ṭbn* und hebräisch *ṭwb* 'Regen': Regenrituale beim Neujahrfest in Kanaan und Israel (Ps 85; 126). *UF* 21:247-258.

Lund, Nils Wilhelm

1932-3 Chiasmus in the Psalms. *American Journal of Semitic Languages and Literatures* 49:281-312.

McDaniel, Thomas F.

1968 Philological Studies in Lamentations. II. *Bib* 49:199-220.

McKane, William

1970 *Proverbs: A New Approach*. London: SCM.

1986 *A Critical and Exegetical Commentary on Jeremiah*, Vol. 1: *Introduction and Commentary on Jeremiah I-XXV*. ICC. Edinburgh: T. & T. Clark.

McKenzie, John L.

1968 *Second Isaiah: Introduction, Translation, and Notes*. AB, Vol. 20. Garden City: Doubleday.

Martinez, Ernest R.

1967 *Hebrew-Ugaritic Index to the Writings of Mitchell J. Dahood: A Bibliography with Indices of Scriptural Passages Hebrew and Ugaritic Words and Grammatical Observations*. Rome: Pontifical Biblical Institute.

1981 *Hebrew-Ugaritic Index II with an Eblaite Index to the Writings of Mitchell J. Dahood: A Bibliography with Indices of Scriptural Passages Hebrew, Ugaritic, and Eblaite Words and Grammatical Observations: Critical Reviews, Doctoral Dissertations and Related Writings*. Subsidia Biblica, Vol. 4. Rome: Pontifical Biblical Institute.

Meyer, Rudolf

1966 *Hebräische Grammatik*, Vol. 2: *Formenlehre Flexionstabellen*. 3rd ed. Berlin: De Gruyter.

1979 Gegensinn und Mehrdeutigkeit in der althebräischen Wort- und Begriffsbildung. *UF* 11:601-612.

Michel, Diethelm

1977 *Grundlegung einer hebräischen Syntax*, Teil 1. *Sprachwissenschaftliche Methodik Genus und Numerus des Nomens*. Neukirchen-Vluyn: Neukirchener Verlag.

Michel, Walter L.

1987 *Job in the Light of Northwest Semitic: Prologue and First Cycle of Speeches Job 1:1 - 14:22*, Vol. 1. BibOr, Vol. 42. Rome: Biblical Institute Press.

Miller, Patrick D.

1970 Apotropaic Imagery in Proverbs 6:20-22. *JNES* 29:129-130.

1979 Vocative Lamed in the Psalter: A Reconsideration. *UF* 11:617-637.

Moran, William L.

1951 New Evidence on Canaanite *taqtul(na)*. *JCS* 5:33-35.

1964 **taqtul* - Third Masculine Singular? *Bib* 45:80-82.

1992 trans. *The Amarna Letters*. Baltimore and London: Johns Hopkins University Press.

Muilenburg, James

1961 The Linguistic and Rhetorical Usages of the Particle כי in the Old Testament. *HUCA* 32:135-160.

Muraoka, Takamitsu

1985 *Emphatic Words and Structures in Biblical Hebrew*. Jerusalem and Leiden: Magnes; Brill.

Müller, Hans-Peter

1994 Nicht-junktiver Gebrauch von *w-* im Althebräischen. *ZAH* 7:141-174.

Niehr, Herbert

1989 צַלְמָוֶת ṣalmāwæt. *In TWAT*, Vol. 6. Col. 1056-1059.

Noegel, Scott B.

1996 Atbash (אתב"ש) in Jeremiah and Its Literary Significance', Part 1. *JBQ* 24:82-89.

North, Christopher R.

1964 *The Second Isaiah*. Oxford: OUP.

Nötscher, Friedrich

1953 Zum emphatischen Lamed. *VT* 3:372-380.

O'Connell, Robert H.

1988 Isaiah xiv 4b-23: Ironic Reversal Through Concentric Structure and Mythic Allusion. *VT* 38:407-418.

O'Connor, M.

1987 The Poetic Inscription from Khirbet el Qôm. *VT* 37:224-230.

Olmo Lete, Gregorio del

1971 Notas críticas al texto hebreo de Jr. 14-17. *Claretianum* 11:283-358.

1981 *Mitos y leyendas de Canaan segun la tradición de Ugarit: textos, versión y estudio*. Fuentes de la ciencia bíblica, Vol. 1. Madrid: Cristiandad.

Oswalt, John N.

1986 *The Book of Isaiah: Chapters 1-39*. NICOT. Grand Rapids: Eerdmans.

Pardee, Dennis G.

1975 The Preposition in Ugaritic (part I). *UF* 7:329-378.

1976 The Preposition in Ugaritic (part II). *UF* 8:215-322.

1977 Attestations of Ugaritic Verb/preposition Combinations in Later Dialects. *UF* 9:205-231.

1984 Ugaritic: Further Studies in Ugaritic Epistolography. *AfO* 31:213-230.

1988 *Les textes para-mythologiques: de la 24e campagne (1961)*. Notice archéologique Jacques-Claude Courtois. Mémoire, Vol. 77. Paris: Recherche sur les Civilisations.

Penar, Tadeusz

1967 'Lamedh Vocativi': Exempla Biblico-hebraica. *Verbum Domini* 45:32-46.

1975 *Northwest Semitic Philology and the Hebrew Fragments of Ben Sira*. BibOr, Vol. 28. Rome: Biblical Institute Press.

Pennacchietti, Fabrizio A.

1974 Appunti per una storia comparata dei sistemi preposizionali semitici. *AION* n.s. 24:161-208.

Pettinato, Giovanni

1981 *The Archives of Ebla: An Empire Inscribed in Clay: With an Afterword by Mitchell J. Dahood, S.J.* Garden City: Doubleday.

Plöger, Otto

1984 *Sprüche Salomos (Proverbia).* BKAT, Vol. 17. Neukirchen: Neukirchener Verlag.

Pope, Marvin H.

1951 Ugaritic Enclitic *-m*. *JCS* 5:123-128.

1973 *Job: Introduction, Translation, and Notes*. 3rd ed. AB, Vol. 15. Garden City: Doubleday.

1977 *Song of Songs: A New Translation with Introduction and Commentary*. AB, Vol. 7C. Garden City: Doubleday.

1988 Vestiges of Vocative *lamedh* in the Bible. *UF* 20:201-207.

Ratner, Robert

1988 Does a *t*- Preformative Third Person Masculine Plural Verbal Form Exist in Biblical Hebrew? *VT* 38:80-88.

1990 The 'feminine Takes Precedence' Syntagm and Job 19,15. *ZAW* 102:238-251.

Ravasi, Gianfranco

1985 *Il libro dei Salmi: commento e attualizzazione*. Testi e commenti, Vol. 1-3. Bologna: Dehoniane.

1992 *Il Cantico dei cantici: commento e attualizzazione*. Testi e commenti, Vol. 4. Bologna: Dehoniane.

Reiter, Karin

1990 Falknerei in Ugarit. *UF* 22:271-278.

Rendsburg, Gary A.

1982 Double Polysemy in Genesis 49:6 and Job 3:6. *CBQ* 44:48-51.

1991 The Strata of Biblical Hebrew. *JNSL* 17:81-99.

1992a Morphological Evidence for Regional Dialects in Ancient Hebrew. *In Linguistics and Biblical Hebrew.* W. Bodine ed. Pp. 65-88. Winona Lake: Eisenbrauns.

1992b Notes on Genesis xv. *VT* 42:266-272.

Rinaldi, Giancarlo

1980 Studi italiani sul testo ebraico anticotestamentario. *Bibbia e Oriente*:55-62.

Ringgren, Helmer

1975 זָנָה *zānaḥ*. *In TWAT*, Vol. 2. Col. 619-621.

Roberts, Bleddyn J.

1962 Athbash. *In IDB*, Vol. 1. Pp. 306-307.

Robertson, David A.

1972 *Linguistic Evidence in Dating Early Hebrew Poetry*. SBLDS, Vol. 3. Missoula: Society of Biblical Literature.

Rudolph, Wilhelm

1968 *Jeremia*. 3rd ed. HAT 1/12. Tübingen: Mohr.

Sabottka, Liudger

1972 *Zephanja: Versuch einer Neuübersetzung mit philologischem Kommentar*. BibOr, Vol. 25. Rome: Biblical Institute Press.

Sanders, James A.

1965 *The Psalms Scroll of Qumrân Cave 11*. DJD, Vol. 4. Oxford: Clarendon.

Sanmartín Ascaso, Joaquín

1973 Semantisches über ʾ*mr*/'sehen' und ʾ*mr*/'sagen' im Ugaritischen. *UF* 5:263-270.

Sarna, Nahum M.

1959 The Interchange of the Prepositions *Beth* and *Min* in Biblical Hebrew. *JBL* 78:310-316.

1963 The Mythological Background of Job 18. *JBL* 82:318.

Sawyer, John F. A.

1974 The 'original Meaning of the Text' and Other Legitimate Subjects of Semantic Description. *In Questions disputées d'Ancient Testament: méthode et théologie*. C.

Brekelmans ed. Pp. 63-70. BETL, Vol. 33. Leuven and Gembloux: Leuven University Press; J. Duculot.

Schmuttermayr, Georg

1971a Ambivalenz und Aspektdifferenz: Bemerkungen zu den hebräischen Präpositionen ב, ל und מן. *BZ* N.F. 15:29-51.

1971b *Psalm 18 und 2 Samuel 22: Studien zu einem Doppeltext: Probleme der Textkritik und Übersetzung und das Psalterium Pianum.* StANT, Vol. 25. München: Kösel.

1985 *Psalm 9-10: Studien zur Textkritik und Übersetzung.* St. Ottilien: EOS.

Schoors, Antoon

1972 Literary Phrases. *In RSP*, Vol. 1. Pp. 1-70.

1973 *I Am God Your Saviour: A Form-critical Study of the Main Genres in Is. XL-LV.* VTS, Vol. 24. Leiden: Brill.

1981 The Particle כי. *OTS* 21:240-276.

1988 A Third Masculine Singular *taqtul* in Biblical Hebrew? *In Text and Context: Old Testament and Semitic Studies for F.C. Fensham.* W. Claassen ed. Pp. 193-200. JSOTS, Vol. 48. Sheffield: JSOT.

Scott, R. B. Y.

1965 *Proverbs. Ecclesiastes: Introduction, Translation, and Notes.* AB, Vol. 18. Garden City: Doubleday.

Segert, Stanislav

1961 Die Sprache der moabitischen Königsinschrift. *ArOr* 29:197-267.

1976 *A Grammar of Phoenician and Punic.* München: Beck.

1984 *A Basic Grammar of the Ugaritic Language: With Selected Texts and Glossary.* Berkeley: University of California Press.

Selms, Adrianus van

1979 The Root *k-ṯ-r* and Its Derivatives in Ugaritic Literature. *UF* 11:739-744.

Singer, A. D.

1948 The Vocative in Ugaritic. *JCS* 2:1-10.

Skehan, Patrick W., and Alexander A. Di Lella

1987 *The Wisdom of Ben Sira: A New Translation with Notes.* AB, Vol. 39. New York: Doubleday.

Smith, John M. P., William H. Ward, and Julius A. Bewer

1912 *A Critical and Exegetical Commentary on Michah, Zephaniah, Nahum, Habakkuk, Obadiah and Joel.* ICC. Edinburgh: T. & T. Clark.

Smith, Ralph L.

1984 *Micah-Malachi.* WBC, Vol. 32. Waco: Word Books.

Stadelmann, Luis

1992 *Love and Politics: A New Commentary on the Song of Songs.* New York: Paulist.

Stec, David M.

1994 *The Text of the Targum of Job: An Introduction and Critical Edition.* AGJU, Vol. 20. Leiden: Brill.

Steiner, Anton

1971 Warum lebten die Essener asketisch? *BZ* 15:1-28.

Steiner, Richard S.

1996 The Two Sons of Neriah and the Two Editions of Jeremiah in the Light of Two *atbash* Code-Words for Babylon. *VT* 46:74-84.

Stuart, Douglas

1987 *Hosea-Jonah.* WBC, Vol. 31. Waco: Word Books.

Sukenik, E.L.

1955 *The Dead Sea Scrolls of the Hebrew University.* Hebrew University Jerusalem: Magnes.

Sutcliffe, Edmund F.

1955 A Note on *ʿal*, *le*, and *from*. *VT* 5:436-439.

Tate, Marvin E.
1990 *Psalms 51-100*. WBC, Vol. 20. Dallas: Word Books.

Thomas, David Winton
1962 צַלְמָוֶת in the Old Testament. *JSS* 7:191-200.

Thompson, John A.
1980 *The Book of Jeremiah*. NICOT. Grand Rapids: Eerdmans.

Tomback, Richard S.
1978 *A Comparative Semitic Lexicon of the Phoenician and Punic Languages*. SBLDS, Vol. 32. Missoula: Scholars.

Toy, Crawford H.
1904 *A Critical and Exegetical Commentary on the Book of Proverbs*. ICC. Edinburgh: T. & T. Clark.

Tromp, Nicholas J.
1969 *Primitive Conceptions of Death and the Netherworld in the Old Testament*. BibOr, Vol. 21. Rome: Pontifical Biblical Institute.

Tuillén Torralba, Juan
1996 Yahvé, mi salvador: Habacuc, 3. *Isidorianum* 10:95-123.

Wagner, S.
1984 מָצָא māṣāʾ. *In TWAT*, Vol. 4. Col. 1043-1063.

Waltke, Bruce K., and M. O'Connor
1990 *An Introduction to Biblical Hebrew Syntax*. Winona Lake: Eisenbrauns.

Ward, William H.
1912 *A Critical and Exegetical Commentary on Michah, Zephaniah, Nahum, Habakkuk, Obadiah and Joel*. ICC. Edinburgh: T. & T. Clark.

Watson, Wilfred G. E.
1972 Archaic Elements in the Language of Chronicles. *Bib* 53:191-207.

1986 *Classical Hebrew Poetry: A Guide to Its Techniques.* 2nd ed. JSOTSS, Vol. 26. Sheffield: JSOT Press.

1990 The Particle *p* in Ugaritic. *SEL* 7:75-86.

1994 Ugaritic *p* Again. *UF* 26:493-495.

Watts, John D. W.

1985 *Isaiah 1-33*. WBC, Vol. 24. Waco: Word Books.

1987 *Isaiah 34-66*. WBC, Vol. 25. Waco: Word Books.

Weiden, W. A. van der

1970 *Le livre des Proverbes: Notes philologiques*. BibOr, Vol. 23. Rome: Pontifical Biblical Institute.

Whitley, Charles F.

1971-2 Some Functions of the Hebrew Particles *beth* and *lamedh*. *JQR* 62:199-206.

Wildberger, Hans

1972 *Jesaja 1. Teilband: Jesaja 1-12*. BKAT, Vol. 10 no. 1. Neukirchen-Vluyn: Neukirchener Verlag.

1978 *Jesaja 2. Teilband: Jesaja 13-27*. BKAT, Vol. 10 no. 2. Neukirchen-Vluyn: Neukirchener Verlag.

1984 *Jesaja 3. Teilband: Jesaja 28-39: das Buch, der Prophet und seine Botschaft*. BKAT, Vol. 10 no. 3. Neukirchen-Vluyn: Neukirchener Verlag.

Wilton, Patrick

1994 More Cases of *waw explicativum*. *VT* 44:125-128.

Wolff, Hans Walter

1965 *Dodekapropheton*, Vol. 1: *Hosea*. 2nd ed. BKAT, Vol. 14, no. 1. Neukirchen-Vluyn: Neukirchener Verlag.

1974 *Hosea: A Commentary on the Book of the Prophet Hosea*. Hermeneia. Philadelphia: Fortress.

1982 *Dodekapropheton*, Vol. 4: *Micha*. BKAT, Vol. 14, no. 4. Neukirchen-Vluyn: Neukirchener Verlag.

Young, Edward J.

1972 *The Book of Isaiah: The English Text, with Introduction, Exposition, and Notes*, Vol. 1: *Chapters 1-18*. 2nd ed. Grand Rapids: Eerdmans.

Young, Ian

1995 The 'northernisms' of the Israelite Narratives in Kings. *ZAH* 8(1):63-70.

Zevit, Ziony

1975 The So-called Interchangeability of the Prepositions *b, l, and m(n)* in Northwest Semitic. *JANES* 7:103-112.

1977 The Linguistic and Contextual Arguments in Support of a Hebrew 3 m.s. Suffix *-y*. *UF* 9:315-328.

Ziegler, Josef

1958 *Beiträge zur Jeremias-Septuaginta*. Göttingen: Vandenhoeck & Ruprecht.

Zimmerli, Walther

1969a *Ezechiel 1. Teilband: Ezechiel 1-24*. BKAT, Vol. 13 no. 1. Neukirchen-Vluyn: Neukirchener Verlag.

1969b *Ezechiel 2. Teilband: Ezechiel 25-48*. BKAT, Vol. 13 no. 2. Neukirchen-Vluyn: Neukirchener Verlag.

1979 *Ezekiel, Vol. 1: A Commentary on the Book of the Prophet Ezekiel Chapters 1-24*. Hermeneia. Philadelphia: Fortress.

1983 *Ezekiel, Vol. 2: A Commentary on the Book of the Prophet Ezekiel Chapters 25-48*. Hermeneia. Philadelphia: Fortress.

Zurro, Eduardo

1987 *Procedimientos iterativos en la poesía ugarítica y hebrea*. BibOr, Vol. 43. Rome: Biblical Institute Press.

Index of Textual Citations

Bible

Genesis

Exodus

Numbers

Deuteronomy

Joshua

Judges

1 Samuel

2 Samuel

1 Kings

2 Kings

1 Chronicles

2 Chronicles

Ezra

Nehemiah

Job

Psalms

Proverbs

Canticle

Isaiah

Jeremiah

Lamentations

Ezekiel

Daniel

Hosea

Qumran

1QIsa[a]

1QIsa[b]

11QPs[a]

El Amarna

El Hofra

KAI

KTU (UT)

Index of Authors

Index of Selected Subjects

Finito di stampare il 21 novembre 1997
Tipografia Poliglotta della Pontificia Università Gregoriana
Piazza della Pilotta, 4 – 00187 Roma

From the same publisher

ANDERSEN, Francis I. – FORBES, A. Dean: The Vocabulary of the Old Testament. First Reprint.
1992. VIII, 724 p. ISBN 88-7653-575-6. L. 85.000

BIBLICA: Index Generalis. Vol. 51-75, 1970-1994.
1997. 140 p. ISSN 006-0887. L. 22.000

BORGER, Rykle: Babylonisch-assyrische Lesestücke. Heft I: Die Texte in Umschrift. – Heft II: Elemente der Grammatik und der Schrift - Glossar - Die Texte in Keilschrift. Erste Nachdruck. (*Analecta Orientalia, 54*).
1994. XII, 352 p. ISBN 88-7653-254-4. L. 50.000

BOZAK, Barbara: Life 'Anew'. A Literary-Theological Study of Jer. 30-31. (*Subsidia Biblica, 122*).
1991. XVIII, 198 p. ISBN 88-7653-122-X. L. 33.500

ČERNÝ, Jaroslav – GROLL, Sarah I., assisted by EYRE, Christopher: A Late Egyptian Grammar. Fourth Edition. (*Studia Pohl. Series Maior, 4*).
1993. LXXXIV, 620 p. ISBN 88-7653-435-0. L. 65.000.

CUNNINGHAM, Graham: 'Deliver me from Evil'. Mesopotamian incantations 2500-1500 BC. (*Studia Pohl - Series Maior, 17*).
1997. VIII, 204 p. ISBN 88-7653-608-6. L. 37.000

DI VITO, Robert A.: Studies in Third Millennium Sumerian and Akkadian Personal Names. The Designation and Conception of the Personal God. (*Studia Pohl - Series Maior, 16*).
1993. XII, 328 p. ISBN 88-7653-601-9. L. 25.000

FITZMYER, Joseph A.: An Introductory Bibliography for the Study of Scripture. Third Revised Edition. (*Subsidia Biblica, 3*).
1990. XVI, 220 p. ISBN 88-7653-592-6. L. 18.500.

FITZMYER, Joseph A.: The Biblical Commission's Document "The Interpretation of the Bible in the Church". Text and Commentary. (*Subsidia Biblica, 18*).
1995. XVI, 212 p. ISBN 88-7653-605-1. L. 30.000

HILL, Robert C.: Breaking the Bread of the Word: Principles of Teaching Scripture. (*Subsidia Biblica, 15*).
1991. XIV, 186 p. ISBN 88-7653-596-9. L. 22.500

JOÜON, Paul – MURAOKA, T.: A Grammar of Biblical Hebrew.
Vol. I: Part One: Orthography and Phonetics.
Part Two: Morphology.
Vol. II: Part Three: Syntax. Paradigms and Indices.
Second Reprint. (*Subsidia Biblica, 14*).
1996. L, 782 p. ISBN 88-7653-595-0. L. 80.000

KOLARCIK, Michael: The Ambiguity of Death in the Book of Wisdom 1-6. A Study of Literary Structure and Interpretation. (*Analecta Biblica, 127*).
1991. XII, 212 p. ISBN 88-7653-127-0. L. 34.500

KUTHIRAKKATTEL, Scaria: The Beginning of Jesus' Ministry according to Mark's Gospel (1,14-3,6): a Redaction Critical Study. (*Analecta Biblica, 123*).
1990. XXVI, 300 p. ISBN 88-7653-123-8. L. 37.000

LENCHAK, Timothy A.: Choose Life! A Rhetorical-Critical Investigation of Deuteronomy 28,69-30,20. (*Analecta Biblica, 129*).
1993. XII, 308 p. ISBN 88-7653-129-7. L. 40.000

MERK, Agostino: Novum Testamentum graece et latine, apparatu critico instructum. Editio undecima.
1992. 48*-1.732 p., 1 tab. ISBN 88-7653-597-7. L. 50.000

NORTH, Robert: Elenchus of Biblica. Vol. 10 (1994).
1997. 1.104 p. ISBN 88-7653-609-4. L. 200.000

O'FEARGHAIL, Fearghus: The Introduction to Luke-Acts. A Study of the Role of Lk. 1,1-4,44 in the Composition of Luke's Two Volume Work. (*Analecta Biblica, 126*).
1991. XII, 256 p. ISBN 88-7653-126-2. L. 38.500

PANIKULAM, George: Koinōnia in the New Testament. A Dynamic Expression of Christian Life. First Reprint. (*Analecta Biblica, 85*).
1994. XII, 164 p. ISBN 88-7653-085-1. L. 22.000

SWETNAM, James: An Introduction to the Study of New Testament Greek. (Part One Morphology).
Vol. I: Lessons.
Vol. II: Key, Lists, Paradigms, Indices. (*Subsidia Biblica, 16*).
1992. LIV, 762 p. ISBN 88-7653-600-0. L. 52.500

VOGT, Ernst: Lexicon linguae aramaicae Veteris Testamenti documentis antiquis illustratum. Altera editio.
1994. 14*-194 p. ISBN 88-7653-548-9. L. 38.000

VOLK, Konrad: A Sumerian Reader. (*Studia Pohl - Series Maior, 18*).
1997. 132 p. ISBN 88-7653-610-8. L. 26.000

VON SODEN, Wolfram – RÖLLIG, Wolfgang: Das akkadische Syllabar. 4., durchgesehene und erweiterte Auflage. (*Analecta Orientalia, 42*).
1991. XLII, 76-24* p. ISBN 88-7653-257-9. L. 40.000

VON SODEN, Wolfram – MAYER, Werner R.: Grundriss der akkadischen Grammatik, 3., ergänzte Auflage. (*Analecta Orientalia, 33*).
1995. XXXII, 328-56* p. ISBN 88-7653-258-7. L. 90.000

ZERWICK, Max – SMITH, Joseph: Biblical Greek. Illustrated by examples. Sixth Reprint.
1994. XVI, 188 p. ISBN 88-7653-554-3. L. 21.000

ZERWICK, Max – GROSVENOR, Mary: A Grammatical Analysis of the Greek New Testament. Fifth Revised Edition.
1996. XXXVIII, 778-16* p. ISBN 88-7653-588-8. L. 50.000

ZORELL, Franz: Lexicon Graecum Novi Testamenti. Editio quarta emendata.
1990. XXIV, (44)-752 p. ISBN 88-7653-590-X. L. 75.000